"Why Race, Prejudice and Racial Discrimination?"

A Construction Based on Jealousy, Pride, Greed, Notions of Superiority and Privilege

Pastor/Apostle K.M. Byam-Brown, Sr.

Edition: First

ISBN: 979-8-89397-858-2

Published by **Twain Book Writers**

Table of Contents

Foreword

Racism, Faith, and Awakening in 1967

Why is humanity divided by race? Where did this thing called "race" come from? What is prejudice, and why do people think that cultures with darker skin are inferior? Who is responsible for the system that encourages discrimination?

I have come to recognize that in very significant ways, I have carried the burden of racism all my life—sometimes as a heavy shadow over my private experiences, other times as a thorn embedded in the practice of my Christian faith. The longer I live, the clearer it becomes that this burden was not simply personal. It was systemic, cultural, and theological. Racism is not an occasional act of prejudice but a structure, a way of ordering the world that defines belonging and exclusion. As Eduardo Bonilla-Silva has argued, racism in the United States is sustained less by explicit hatred than by the "color-blind" norms and practices that make racial inequality appear natural or inevitable (Bonilla-Silva 2).

My own experience confirms this. Even before I could name what was happening, I felt the sting of prejudice. It was present in the rituals and exclusions of the Shriners and the Scottish Rite in my hometown. It was evident in the subtleties of everyday life—the sidelong glances, the veiled remarks, the small but cutting reminders that belonging was not equally shared. These were not isolated incidents but expressions of a hierarchy of race that had been erected long before I was born.

The Normalization of Racism

For years I accepted the racial striation (lines, scratches and grooves that form in a parallel pattern on a surface, resulting from various natural or artificial processes) as the natural order of things. Racism was not presented to me as cruelty but disguised as order - as tradition and "the way things are." This is precisely what Bonilla-Silva calls the "normalcy of racism," where inequality is maintained not through overt racial violence but through cultural assumptions that seem ordinary (Bonilla-Silva 9). I was too young, and too deeply socialized to question it.

The church, too, played a role in this normalization. I was not raised in an overly-Christian environment, but I attended my neighborhood's churches and was Episcopalian, Presbyterian and United Methodist in my childhood. The church spoke about love and forgiveness but rarely, if ever, about justice or the systemic exclusion of Black Americans. I was way too young to know what was going on when there was protesting about closing a YMCA, having a large black and neighborhood constituency. Although there was another one built in our neighborhood to appease the controversial situation, I still lacked understanding of what was actually going on.

Theologian James Cone later gave me the language I had lacked as a child. In Black Theology and Black Power, Cone declared that "any message that is not related to the liberation of the poor in a society is not Christ's message" (Cone 35). But as a boy, I never acquired tools to perceive the contradictions between its proclamation of the gospel and its silence in the face of racial injustice from the church. That, actually, only came from some radical Black Muslims and the Nation of Islam; amassing black youth in our neighborhood and urging us to come to some of their evening gatherings.

1967–68: A Shattering of Illusion

The years 1967 and 1968 shattered the illusion. These were the years of the *"long, hot summers,"* when racial uprisings swept across dozens of American cities in response to police brutality, poverty, and systemic exclusion. In 1967 alone, there were more than 150 urban uprisings; the most notable in Detroit and Newark (Sugrue 221).

I can still recall my own moment of confrontation with this reality - running down the cracked asphalt of my neighborhood street, my heart pounding as a group of black men surged through town in protest. I was terrified—not because of what they might do to me, but because I had no idea why they were there and protesting. No one had explained to me the history of their anger, the depth of their grievances or the urgency of their cries. To me, their fury came out of nowhere.

What I failed to understand, then, was that these protests were not sudden explosions of rage. They were, as Dr. Martin Luther King Jr. observed, *"the language of the unheard"* (*Why We Can't Wait* 293). The men I saw marching were part of a much larger struggle - one that stretched back through slavery, Jim Crow, segregation and economic marginalization. My fear in that moment was not about the protesters themselves but about my ignorance. I had mistaken the cries of justice for chaos, when in truth, they were the sound of centuries of inequality breaking into public view.

Systemic Racism and White Blindness

As I look back, I see that moment as a lesson in the power of systemic racism. *Racism does not only oppress those directly harmed by it—it also blinds those outside its path to the reasons behind resistance.* My ignorance that day was not an accident. It was the product of a culture that shielded me from the truth. As Ibram X. Kendi argues in *How to Be an Antiracist, racism is not just about personal animus but about structures that create and defend racial hierarchies* (Kendi 18). Those structures had kept me from seeing clearly.

James Baldwin captured this dynamic with searing clarity. In *The Fire Next Time*, he wrote: *"The root of the Negro problem is the necessity of the white man to find a way of living with the Negro in order to live with himself"* (Baldwin 67). My oblivion to the issues of race was not neutral—it was a mechanism of self-preservation for white identity. It kept us comfortable by keeping us ignorant.

Faith and Complicity

The theological dimension of this blindness is perhaps the hardest for me to reckon with. Christianity was central to my upbringing, yet I never confronted racism head-on through the church. Instead, my casual involvement sanctified the very traditions that sustained racial inequality. Kelly Brown Douglas, in her book *Stand Your Ground: Black Bodies and the Justice of God*, has argued that *American Christianity has been deeply entangled with a "stand-your-ground" culture that devalues black life and sacralizes white identity* (Douglas 45). Reading her work later in life, I recognized echoes of my own experience.

James Cone put the matter even more starkly: *"The scandal is not so much that white Christians are oppressors, but that they are oblivious to their oppression"* (*A Black Theology of Liberation* 64). My churches did not see themselves as an "activist" church. They saw themselves as respectable, orderly and moral. Yet by failing to name and resist systemic racism, they became complicit in its continuation.

Toward Awakening

It took years for me to begin unlearning what I had been sensitized to think was normal. The civil rights movement itself was one teacher. Dr. Martin Luther King Jr.'s *Letter from Birmingham Jail* spoke with prophetic clarity to people like me, believing that gradual change or silence was preferable to confrontation. *"Shallow understanding from people of good will is more frustrating than absolute misunderstanding from people of ill will"* (King 296). In those words, I recognized myself.

The Black Liberation theologians and anti-racist scholars I encountered later, gave me the tools to name what I had experienced and what I had failed to see. Christina Edmondson and Chad Brennan, in *Faithful Antiracism*, argue that *the church must move "past talk to systemic change"* (14). Programs like JustFaith Ministries' *Faith and Racial Justice* now invite Christians to see racism, not simply as an individual

4

sin, but as a structural reality embedded in education, housing, policing and the church itself (JustFaith Ministries).

When I look back at the frightened child running down the street in 1967, I see more than fear. I see the beginnings of an awakening. I see a boy shaped by a culture of blindness - taught to misinterpret justice as chaos, but also one who would one day begin to glimpse the truth. The voices I once perceived as threatening were, in fact, voices of truth calling for freedom long denied.

As Baldwin warned, America could either face this truth or risk *"the fire next time."* As a person of faith, I now see that my calling is not to deny or diminish the cries of the oppressed, but to hear them as the Holy Spirit's own voice. Racism blinds, but truth—painful, urgent, disruptive truth—can still open eyes.

Introduction

Mr. Gross – The "Debit Man"

It was a quiet Saturday morning—ordinary, predictable, the kind of morning when the rhythms of family life moved in familiar ways. Around nine or ten o'clock, Mr. Gross arrived. In our neighborhood, men like him were known as debit men. They went door-to-door each week, collecting coins and small bills from families who had purchased clothing or small "whole life" insurance policies.

These policies were never designed to build wealth, pay for college, or leave an inheritance. Their purpose was narrow and stark: to cover the cost of burial. The clothing these debit men sold were well-made and stylish, the kind of garments people admired—but priced far beyond what most Black families, especially Black women, could reasonably afford.

The companies sold these items at steep markups, offering the illusion of luxury through installment payments collected every two weeks or on payday. It was a system that looked like an opportunity but functioned as exploitation. The debit men and their employers profited handsomely, while Black women paid dearly for the right to wear elegance—even when it came at an inflated cost.

For many Black families, these clothes and insurance policies were the only "luxuries" available. Prominent companies like Prudential and Mutual of Omaha—household names that preached family values on programs like Wild Kingdom—refused to ensure Black families at levels comparable to white ones (Heen 391). Despite our loyalty as viewers, despite our payments, we remained excluded. Clothing (such as the items sold by the debit men) was already priced too high in the retail stores, so circuit debit men sold at a higher cost on a "colored credit" basis.

We called it colored credit because the debit men came every other week, carrying ledgers thick with the names of families like ours. They went door to door, collecting coins and crumpled bills for clothing and burial insurance that promised dignity we could afford only in installments. Mr. Gross was one of them—polite enough, always respectful—but his visits carried the weight of something heavier: a reminder of how the world had arranged itself against us.

For many Black women, these visits meant more than simply paying a bill. They were a measure of standing—a sign that you were responsible, respectable, holding your own even when the odds said otherwise. To fall behind was to risk shame, not only before the debit man, but before the neighborhood. Yet the bitter truth remained: the beautiful clothes, with their fine stitching and rich fabrics, cost far more than they were worth. The companies knew what they were selling—dignity at a markup—and they knew we would buy it.

Black women, and other women of color, paid faithfully during those times; not because they were fooled, but because they understood what was at stake. To walk into work or church in a freshly pressed dress wasn't vanity; it was resistance. It was a declaration of worth in a world determined to deny it. Every pressed seam, every polished shoe, every starched collar was an act of quiet defiance—a way of saying, I am somebody.

But the cost was steep. Week after week, money that could have gone toward savings or children's needs went instead into the hands of the debit men. These were not banks or fair credit institutions; they were trapdoors disguised as opportunity. Hardworking Black families paid and paid, and when the garments wore out or the insurance matured, there was nothing left to show but the memory of having looked like we belonged—even if only for a moment.

Looking back, I see how complicated it all was. The debit system offered access, but only on terms that kept Black people in their place. It allowed us to look the part of progress while quietly draining the wealth that could have made progress real. And yet, through it all, Black women carried themselves with grace. They transformed exploitation into elegance, scarcity into style. Even as they paid the price, they refused to be defined by what they owed.

That is the paradox of colored credit: it took from us, but it could not take our pride. It reminded us that even when the system was stacked against us, we still found ways to look, live, and love as though we had already won.

The justification for our exclusion was wrapped in the sterile language of actuarial "risk," but its foundation was racism. Black people were labeled early-death prone—a phrase born not of data, but of prejudice. Insurers claimed that poverty, poor health, and "irresponsibility," supposedly endemic to Black culture, made us too great a liability. To them, investing in Black life was never profitable, because they assumed our lives would be cut short, fragile, and expendable (Sowell 214; Heen 393). What was presented as objective mathematics was, in truth, systemic racism dressed in business attire.

This one particular Saturday, that system's cruelty revealed itself in a single gesture. Mr. Gross, after collecting that visit's debit from my parents, reached out as if he were going to pat my father on the head. My father stopped and cautioned him, and his hand fell with casual authority of someone ready to discipline a child or indulge a pet. It was almost like a "good boy" gesture. I was five years old, but the insult cracked the air. My father's body went rigid; his face hardened into something I had never seen before—rage, sudden and silent. For a moment, I thought violence might erupt. But it didn't. He held himself back, forcing his fury inward. Mr. Gross left with his pockets full of our money and his condescension intact.

When the door closed, my father exhaled one word: "Whitey." It wasn't playful or performative; it was the language of resistance, spoken under his breath because open defiance was too dangerous. That word burned into my memory. It was the moment I first understood that something sacred had been violated. My father—who to me was strength itself— had been demeaned and forced to swallow his anger to keep our family safe.

Years later, I came to understand that what I witnessed was not an isolated insult but a symptom of a much larger system. Scholars have shown how "colored credit," insurance companies, banks, and real estate firms together built the economic cage that confined Black families. They didn't merely reflect inequality—they engineered it, ensuring that entire communities were denied the wealth-building tools freely available to white America (Schweikart 59).

Mr. Gross was more than a collector of payments. He was an agent of that system, a man who delivered its message in person: that Black lives were to be measured, priced, and collected in installments—one garment, one policy, one humiliation at a time.

That Saturday morning remains etched in my memory. It was my first lesson in how racism works—not only through slurs and violence, but through contracts, premiums, and the everyday transactions of life. It was also my first glimpse of the psychological cost of survival: the way Black men like my father carried their rage behind a mask of restraint, because to resist too openly was to risk everything.

Systemic Racism and Insurance Discrimination

In retrospect, Mr. Gross's visits were not only personal memories but historical evidence. Historians have traced how life insurance companies systematically excluded black families from wealth-building financial products. While white families were offered whole life and term policies that accumulated cash value and provided intergenerational security, black families were relegated to *"burial insurance"* that did nothing beyond cover death *(Heen 389)*. This exclusion effectively foreclosed opportunities for economic mobility, locking communities of color out of one of the key instruments of middle-class stability.

This practice, now referred to as "actuarial racism" - *a term used to describe situations where actuarial methods (the statistical models and risk classifications used in insurance and finance) contribute to, reinforce, or justify racial inequities* - demonstrates how prejudice was encoded into financial systems. By embedding existing social inequalities—*poverty, segregated housing, limited access to healthcare*—into actuarial tables, companies justified excluding black clients and other clients of color, while claiming neutrality *(Schweikart 56)*. In doing so, they transformed discrimination into policy, turning racial stereotypes into *"data"* and inequality into profit.

My father's humiliation at the hands of Mr. Gross, cannot be read as a single moment of disrespect. It was a visible scar of a larger structure—an industry that diminished black humanity while reinforcing white security. The pat on the head was not merely insulting – it was the local enactment of a national system that consistently rendered black life less valuable, less secure, and less insurable.

The Question of Racism and the Milton Hershey School Experience

"Where did racism come from?" I remember asking myself that question many years later as an adult - long after I had first encountered its sting. My experience with racism was never singular. It appeared in multiple forms - sometimes subtle, sometimes unmistakably harsh. As a teenager, I, without really thinking about it, participated in segregated activities. It was only in retrospect that I realized how thoroughly these divisions had been normalized. Later, it was at Milton Hershey School in the early 1970s that the question became unavoidable, sharpening into a persistent and uncomfortable awareness.

As a thirteen-year-old boy arriving at Milton Hershey School, I was immediately struck by the school's dual nature. On the surface, Milton Hershey School seemed to be a beacon of opportunity - a residential school promising education, community, and structure for children losing their parents in death and from financially vulnerable socio-economic backgrounds. My father had passed away one year prior to my arrival, and my mother did not want me to be in the public, urban school system. Yet beneath the promises, the school reflected the broader social tensions of a post–Civil Rights America. Although overt segregation had been legally outlawed, informal racial hierarchies still persisted. Graduating classes, student homes across divisions and extra-curricular activities often carried unspoken lines of division. Black students were largely ignored in academic and social contexts, except when it came to sports like football, basketball, and wrestling. There was a small number of us breaking the color line in the 60's and 70's, and white students carried the tacit privileges of proximity to mainstream culture. (Feagan 26).

In the early 1970s, the United States was grappling with the aftermath of major civil rights legislation. The Civil Rights Act of 1964 and the Voting Rights Act of 1965 had legally dismantled Jim Crow, but de facto

11

segregation persisted in education, housing, and American neighborhoods. Schools like Milton Hershey School *(even though they were private schools)* existed at the intersection of these social forces. Nationwide, busing policies were creating tension in urban and suburban districts, white flight was reshaping neighborhoods, and affirmative action initiatives were beginning to challenge entrenched racial hierarchies (Orfield and Lee 19). Within this larger national context, the Milton Hershey School became a microcosm of the challenges facing American institutions attempting to reconcile ideals of equality with entrenched racial attitudes.

For me, the experience was both illuminating and confounding. I witnessed the subtle ways in which racial bias operated - classrooms were not as diverse as the public school I was accustomed to, and the attempt to approach world history from an Afro-Asian perspective did not speak to global diversity or Black History in a way that could be meaningful. There were no real discussions about race, and those who were selected for leadership roles *(class president, Headmasters, and National Honor Society)* in the school were white. Discipline was corporal punishment and detentions for even minor infractions, and the social codes of acceptance and belonging were often coded in whiteness; a dynamic described by Joe Feagin as the *"white racial frame"*—a cultural lens that normalizes white perspectives while marginalizing others (Feagin 26). I was living inside that frame, a participant in its privileges and a witness to its exclusions.

At the same time, Christian teaching pervaded the school in religious education. We were instructed in ideals of unity and moral integrity, yet these lessons often clashed with the social realities around us. While the school preached universal values and initiated an ecumenical worship service, it operated within a cultural and structural context that tacitly reinforced racial hierarchies. Theologian Kelly Brown Douglas has argued that *American Christianity has frequently aligned itself with whiteness, using religious authority to sanctify social inequalities and render systemic racism invisible* (Douglas 59). This tension—*the contrast between preached values and lived experience*—created a subtle cognitive dissonance that I only began to untangle in adulthood.

As a teenager, my prior participation in segregated intramural activities illustrated how deeply internalized these divisions had become. I did not question the norms of exclusion when I was picked last because the activity needed to have an extra participant. I accepted them as naturally being a part of the environment, and it was only later, reflecting as an adult, that I realized how profoundly these experiences had shaped my understanding of race. I began to see that racism is not simply an external force to be observed in slurs or violence—it is embedded in culture, in institutions, and in everyday practices that seem neutral or inevitable.

The broader historical context illuminates why these patterns persisted. Despite legislative victories, the 1970s remained a decade of contested integration. School districts implemented busing to promote racial balance, yet white resistance often undermined these efforts. Housing patterns reinforced segregation, and access to economic resources remained unevenly distributed (Orfield and Lee 19). In this environment, institutions like Milton Hershey School were caught between their stated ideals and the prevailing social norms, producing environments where racism could operate subtly, structurally, and psychologically.

This awareness of systemic injustice eventually deepened my understanding of the theological dimension of racism. Christianity had encouraged me to seek justice, yet the church and religious institutions often remained complicit in maintaining inequality. James Cone, in *Black Theology and Black Power*, explains that religious teachings must confront the realities of oppression to be authentic: *"Any message that is not related to the liberation of the poor in a society is not Christ's message"* (Cone 35). I began to see that the racial inequities I witnessed at Milton Hershey School were not separate from moral responsibility— they were part of the same struggle for justice that the gospel demanded.

Ultimately, asking the question, *"Where did racism come from?"* led me to understand that it is both historical and structural - personal and systemic. My experiences as a student at Milton Hershey School revealed how legal desegregation did not automatically translate into social equality; how subtle hierarchies persisted and how institutions— *educational, financial, religious*—can reinforce inequality even while espousing noble ideals. These lessons laid the groundwork for a lifelong process of reflection, unlearning, and engagement with questions of justice, faith, and moral responsibility.

Reflections on Faith, Race, and the Genealogy of Jesus

Over fifty years ago, I gave my life to Jesus Christ. It was an experience that introduced me to the profound revelation and theology of the Kingdom of God. Salvation was, for me, a radical new beginning. Understanding myself as a *"new creation"* in Christ (2 Corinthians 5:17) and the kingdom of God, fundamentally reshaped not only my personal identity, but also my understanding of the world. In the kingdom of God, we are the sons of God and the eradication of an old nature and the infusion of the "divine nature," for me, transcends race. We are like Jesus – spiritual and do not know ourselves or anyone else "after the flesh." (2 Corinthians 5) It was as though the lens through which I had viewed life—*its divisions, hierarchies, and assumptions*—had been replaced with a perspective oriented toward justice, reconciliation, and spiritual unity.

Even as I embraced this new faith, the question of race continued to press upon me because many of my contemporary and evangelical counterparts did not share the same understanding. As a senior at Milton Hershey, I vividly remember a white classmate asking me whether I believed that the *"race question"* would be resolved in our lifetime. I answered with caution and hope, because I had already witnessed the deep anxieties many of my peers carried about interracial relationships.

Some concluded that children of such unions would bear a social burden, inheriting prejudice from all sides. Others were totally against "inter-mixing" and could never accept one of their children "coming home" with a black person, or having grandchildren of color. Ironically, this is exactly what happened in their families later on in their adult years. So, the dialogue that was seemingly casual at that time lingered in my mind for decades and raised new questions about differences in theology, spiritual and cultural identity, equity, and the ways racial hierarchies persist even among believers in Christ.

My engagement with Kingdom theology and contemporary evangelical and Pentecostal Christian faith often left me in tension. I witnessed racial anger in the Black Church, and the discomfort that black Christian believers had with white people coming to their churches, participating in their religious meetings. I cringed when black leaders would speak of their disapproval of white cultural norms, empathizing with white people and feeling that they were being disrespected and insulted. Ironically, black church leaders would acquiesce to a "softer tone" in rhetoric, fearing white retaliation if they spoke out too forcefully. Yet, on the other hand, if a white person showed up in support of their programs, it somehow legitimized their efforts.

I had a faith that taught love, unity, and justice, yet I lived in a society structured around racial division. It was during seminary, in the study of scripture, that a deeper theological curiosity began to shape my reflection. I realized that Jesus himself was a person of color, historically, and ethnically rooted in the Jewish people of first-century Palestine. He was part of a genealogy that reflected the diversity and complexity of God's people and was far removed from the Eurocentric, white-washed depictions I had encountered in paintings by Warner Sallman, stained glass, and popular media (Ehrman 45).

This realization prompted a series of questions that connected faith, scripture, and the historical construction of race. I began to wonder how the image of a white Jesus had become so normalized in American

Christianity. If Jesus' genealogy was both ethnically and historically accurate, what did this reveal about the theological claims of racial hierarchy? Scholars such as *Wilson (2014)* have argued that the *"white Jesus"* was a cultural and political construct, serving to reinforce European notions of superiority while obscuring the Jewish and Middle Eastern context of the biblical narrative.

From there, my curiosity deepened into genealogical and even mythological considerations. In some traditions, Japheth is described as one of Noah's sons and considered the progenitor of European or *"white"* peoples (Genesis 10:2–5). Because I was also told that the genealogy of Jesus is inclusive of all peoples, regardless of race, this raised more provocative questions for me, *"Given that the genealogy of Jesus in Matthew 1:1–16 and Luke 3:23–38 roots him in the House of David, and acknowledging that Christian tradition affirms the inclusivity of all peoples in Christ, does the biblical record of his ancestry include descendants of Japheth? If not, how should we understand cultural portrayals of Jesus—such as the common 'white Jesus' image—in light of both his historical Jewish identity and the universal significance attributed to him by the Church?"* While scripture emphasizes Jesus' Jewish ancestry through Judah and David, the broader historical and mythological lineages associated with Noah's sons suggest that racial categorization, as constructed in later centuries, does not align with biblical genealogies.

This line of questioning is not merely historical curiosity—it intersects with theology and social ethics. If Jesus, the incarnate Son of God, was ethnically Jewish and not white, then the pervasive depiction of Him as white reveals a significant distortion in the cultural imagination of the Church. James Cone, in *The Cross and the Lynching Tree*, argues that such distortions of the image of Christ have profound implications for social justice – *"...when Jesus is depicted in the likeness of the dominant culture, marginalized peoples may struggle to see themselves as part of God's kingdom (Cone 2011, 36)."*

My reflections have led me to consider that questions of race, scripture, and representation are inseparable from the lived reality of the Christian faith. Recognizing Jesus as a person of color, embedded in the genealogical and cultural history of the Jewish people, challenges Eurocentric notions of divinity and authority. It also invites a broader theological and ethical reflection: *"If God became human within a marginalized community, then isn't the Kingdom of God calling all believers to confront oppression and racial injustice in our world."* (Cone 35)

Ultimately, this exploration bridges personal faith, historical inquiry, and social consciousness. My early hope that racial reconciliation might occur within my lifetime now extends into a deeper understanding - *the work of justice is ongoing, grounded not only in law or policy, but also in the faithful recognition of God's incarnation in the life of a historically and ethnically situated Jesus.* It compels me to question inherited images, to confront systemic distortions, and to advocate for a Kingdom of God where all human lives, regardless of color or ancestry, are fully recognized and valued.

Jesus, Race and the Lineage of Shem

As I continued to explore my faith in seminary, one question kept returning to me – *"Jesus' identity in a world so preoccupied with race?"* I had long accepted the images I grew up with—*paintings, stained glass windows, depictions of Jesus as a fair-skinned, blue-eyed man.* But the more I studied scripture, the more I realized that these depictions were cultural inventions rather than historical realities. So, I began to trace Jesus' ancestry, and what I found was both illuminating and clarifying. **There is no descendant of Japheth in Jesus' genealogy** according to the Gospels of Matthew and Luke. Both genealogies trace His lineage through Shem - the son of Noah, not Japheth or Ham. I had to stop and consider the weight of this - the biblical Jesus comes from the line of Abraham, rooted in the Semitic peoples of the ancient Near East, not from the European line of Japheth (Genesis 11:10–26).

I remember laying out the genealogy in front of me, almost like a family tree, and seeing it step by step. Noah had three sons - Shem, the ancestor of *Hebrews, Arabs, and Assyrians;* Ham, the ancestor of *Egyptians, Canaanites, and various African and Near Eastern groups*; and Japheth, the progenitor of *Indo-European peoples (who are later identified as "white")—the Greeks, Persians, Medes, and eventually Europeans* (Genesis 10:1–5). Jesus' line, I realized, flows through Shem and Abraham, David and Judah—deeply rooted in the Jewish people.

This revelation changed how I saw everything. The white-washed images of Jesus I had absorbed since childhood were not merely inaccurate; they were misleading in profound ways. Scholars like *Bart Ehrman* note that these *Eurocentric depictions served to align Christ with the dominant culture rather than historical reality (Ehrman 45).* *Jonathan Wilson* echoes this, arguing that the *"white Jesus"* is a cultural artifact, designed to reinforce European notions of racial and social authority *(Wilson 33–58).*

For me, understanding Jesus as a Semitic Jew made the racial questions I had wrestled with my whole life feel more urgent and intimate, because the person I believed in and the Savior I trusted was not white. H*e was part of a marginalized, oppressed people, just like me!* That insight transformed my reflections on faith, justice, and race. It underscored the truth that *God enters human history in the lives of the vulnerable, the colonized, the disenfranchised—not the privileged.* And yet, it also raised a question I had never considered before seminary: *"If Jesus is depicted as white in so much of Western art and culture, what does that mean for the ways the Church has represented authority and divinity? What does it mean for those of us seeking justice in a world still structured by racial hierarchies?"* The answer, I realized, is that faith requires attention to both historical truth and moral responsibility. Seeing Jesus in His proper ethnic and cultural context compels us to confront injustice wherever it is hidden, even when it is subtle, even when it is in the images we have long accepted as sacred.

The Hamitic Line in the Genealogy of Jesus:
Rahab and Divine Inclusion

Then, something unexpected and fascinating happened. As I studied the genealogies of Jesus, a revelation came forth that ultimately inspired the title of this book, *"Why Race, Prejudice, and Racial Discrimination?" "Since Luke 3:23–38 traces Jesus' genealogy back to Adam, passing through Shem (Luke 3:36) but not Japheth, and since the Messianic covenant was carried through Shem's line—through Abraham, Isaac, Jacob, Judah, and David—fulfilling God's promises to Israel (Genesis 12:1–3; 2 Samuel 7:12–16), how should we understand the human construction of 'race'? If Scripture emphasizes covenant rather than ethnicity, why is humanity categorized by race at all, and why do we continue to struggle with prejudice and racial discrimination?"*

Amidst this carefully preserved Semitic lineage, one figure stands out as a remarkable exception – Rahab the harlot, and the Canaanite woman who played a pivotal role in the story of Joshua and the conquest of Jericho (Joshua 2:1–21). Rahab's inclusion in the genealogy of Jesus, as recorded in Matthew 1:5, is striking not only for its historical and cultural implications but also for what it reveals about God's radical vision of inclusion. As a Canaanite, Rahab is traditionally associated with Ham and not Shem. Through her marriage into Israel and the birth of her son Boaz, a Hamitic line is incorporated into the Messianic covenant - a lineage that includes King David and ultimately Jesus Christ. This intersection of lineages carries profound theological and social meaning. Scholars such as *Amy-Jill Levine* have emphasized that the inclusion of women like Rahab, Tamar, Ruth, and Bathsheba in Jesus' genealogy signals a deliberate challenge to social and ethnic boundaries (Levine 92). By weaving Rahab—a descendant of Ham, a foreigner and a former outsider—into the ancestry of the Messiah, the biblical narrative undermines rigid racial and ethnic exclusivity. Rahab's story demonstrates that God's purposes transcend human constructions of race, nationality, and cultural purity.

From a historical perspective, Rahab's inclusion also highlights the complex ways in which the ancient Israelites interacted with neighboring peoples. As a Canaanite, Rahab was initially part of a community often depicted as hostile to Israel, yet her faith and allegiance led to her integration into God's covenantal plan (Miller 214). The genealogical record, therefore, is not merely a static list of names but a dynamic testimony to God's capacity to redeem and incorporate diverse peoples into the divine plan. Theologically, this has implications for understanding race, inclusion, and justice in the context of the Kingdom of God. Just as Rahab, a Hamitic woman, was embraced into the Messianic line, the gospel calls believers to see beyond the artificial barriers of race and ethnicity, prejudice, and cultural hierarchy. James Cone writes that the God revealed in Jesus Christ is a *God who identifies with the marginalized and the oppressed, often subverting social expectations to bring justice and reconciliation* (Cone 35). Rahab's story is a biblical precedent for this radical inclusivity.

In my reflection, I realized that the genealogy of Jesus is not simply a matter of historical record or theological formality; it is also a profound commentary on human social constructs, including race. Even in an ancestry carefully traced through Shem, God deliberately incorporates a line from Ham, revealing that the divine vision is broader, more inclusive, and radically countercultural. It is this pattern—*of God moving across boundaries, integrating the outside, and valuing the marginalized*—that underpins my ongoing exploration of race, prejudice, and discrimination in the human story.

The Hamitic Hypothesis and the Misuse of Scripture

It was during my time in seminary, that I first encountered and learned about the **Hamitic Hypothesis** - *a theological and pseudo-historical interpretation of Genesis 9:26–27*. It had far-reaching consequences for the construction of race and social hierarchies compared to what I had previously understood. In Genesis 9:26–27, Noah blesses his sons after the Flood....*"Blessed be the Lord, the God of Shem. May God enlarge Japheth, and may he dwell in the tents of Shem, and may Canaan be his servant."* He did this because he had been shamed by Ham, his youngest son. Ham encountered him intoxicated from the wine he had indulged in from his vineyard, and as he was passed out from the inebriation and naked, Ham went and told his brothers Shem and Japheth, encouraging them to come and shame their father too, but they refused. Thus, Noah pronounces a blessing over Shem and Japheth and a curse over Canaan, Ham's son.

The narrative of Noah's drunkenness and Ham's actions is central to what later came to be called the **Hamitic Hypothesis**, a *misinterpretation historically used to justify racial hierarchies.* The text records that Ham failed to protect his father's dignity, rather than covering Noah as Shem and Japheth did. He publicized his father's shame, and Rashi interprets Ham's act as seeing Noah's disgrace and then telling his brothers *"with derision, in the street,"* making his sin one of mockery and disrespect (Rashi on Gen. 9:22). Rabbinic traditions, however, deepen the gravity of Ham's actions. Some rabbis suggest that Ham castrated Noah so that he could not have more children, thus attacking Noah's future and inheritance (Sanhedrin 70a). "Some rabbis taught that Ham's act of 'seeing his father's nakedness' was not just about looking, but a biblical way of saying he committed a sexual offense against Noah." (Sanhedrin 70a). This would explain the severity of the curse that followed.

In contrast, Shem and Japheth acted with reverence, walking backwards with their eyes averted as they covered Noah with a garment (Gen. 9:23). The Midrash teaches that because Shem led in honoring Noah, his descendants—the Israelites—were rewarded with the mitzvah of tzitzit, a sacred garment, while Japheth's descendants received the dignity of proper burial (Bereishit Rabbah 36:6). By contrast, Ham's degradation of his father became the grounds for Noah's curse upon Ham's son Canaan.

The **Hamitic Hypothesis** later *misread this biblical and rabbinic tradition, extending Noah's curse on Canaan to all the descendants of Ham,* and *using it to rationalize the enslavement and oppression of African peoples.* Jewish tradition, however, situates Ham's failure not in race or ethnicity, but in his breach of filial respect, modesty, and human dignity.

At first glance, the passage seems straightforward—a prophetic blessing that sets the trajectory for the descendants of Shem, Ham, and Japheth. Yet *over centuries, some interpreters warped its meaning. They suggested that Japheth - traditionally associated with the progenitor of Indo-European (white) peoples, would benefit from and dwell in the spiritual blessings of Shem - the ancestor of the Semitic peoples, while simultaneously elevating Japheth's line as superior to others.* This reading was then used to justify European (white) dominance over non-European peoples (people of color) and, critically, to sanction the enslavement, colonization, and oppression of African (black), Indigenous (native American), and non-European populations.

This misuse of scripture became formalized in what came to be called the **Hamitic Hypothesis**, *a racial theory popularized in the 19th and early 20th centuries.* It further claimed that all **advanced civilizations** in Africa—*Egyptians, Ethiopians, Nubians*—were the descendants of Ham, cursed by Noah; while the white European line of Japheth was divinely favored to rule over others. Historian *Geraldine Heng* observes that such interpretations *"recast biblical narrative into a tool of imperial* *and racial ideology, creating a hierarchy of peoples that justified European conquest and the global slave trade"* (Heng 102).

Contemporary scholarship has exposed the theological and ethical flaws of this ideology. *Catherine Keller* notes that the **Hamitic Hypothesis** *"represents one of the clearest examples of exegesis turned into ideology - a text meant to describe post-Flood familial relations is transformed into a pseudo-scientific justification for racial domination"* (Keller 87). Indeed, what was a genealogical blessing in scripture was twisted into a moral rationale for racial hierarchy, privilege, and oppression, embedding structural inequalities into law, culture, **and religion for centuries.**

Reflecting on this in seminary, I was struck by how deeply scripture could be manipulated to reinforce existing social structures. I was thankful that I resolved my struggle with Biblical Interpretation 101 during my first and second years in seminary, and the exegetical methods of critical analysis. Noah's words—blessing Shem, promising that Japheth would "dwell in his tents"—were *co-opted to promote a sense of European (white) superiority and a spiritualized justification for colonialism and slavery.* Sociologist *Anthony Appiah* observes that such reinterpretations illustrate how *texts can be deployed not to illuminate truth but to maintain systems of power, legitimizing the subjugation of entire peoples through what appears to be divine sanction (Appiah 45).*

Understanding this history transformed the way I approach scripture, theology, and social ethics. The misuse of **Genesis 9:26–27** was not merely a historical curiosity—it was *a cautionary tale about how religious texts could be weaponized to justify racism, classism, and cultural domination.* It also underscored the importance of critically reading scripture in its historical and literary context, while resisting ideological readings that elevate one group over another.

For me, the text became very clear - *the blessings of Shem were never intended as a tool of oppression for Japheth's descendants. They were part of a covenantal promise that emphasized relationship, moral responsibility, and stewardship, not domination.* The centuries-long distortion of this text reminds us that faith and scripture are inseparable from ethical reflection, and that theological interpretation carries moral weight—especially when it shapes systems of power, privilege, and oppression in human society.

The Curse of Ham and the Construction of Global Racism

It troubled me deeply when I came to realize that there was no biblical curse of Ham; the curse was pronounced upon Canaan alone – Ham's son- and that the narrative in scripture, concerning the descendants of Canaan, *was systematically exploited to justify centuries of human oppression.* The story, found in Genesis 9:20–27, was abstract and genealogical in its original context. Yet over time, *interpreters and colonizers transformed it into a pseudo-theological rationale for slavery, racial hierarchy, and global domination.* In the **Americas,** this *misreading became a cornerstone of the Trans-Atlantic Slave Trade, providing moral and religious cover for the brutal enslavement of African peoples.* Historian *Geraldine Heng* observes that the curse of Ham *"functioned as a scriptural warrant for violence and dispossession, enabling Europeans to construct hierarchies that naturalized subjugation"* (Heng 105).

The ideology did not remain localized. *Explorers, traders, and colonial administrators carried it across continents.* The African expeditions of Lewis and Clark, though primarily geographic and commercial in focus, were informed by a worldview steeped in **racialized hierarchies -** *a worldview that presumed European (white) cultural and moral superiority* (Saunt 72). This **pseudo-biblical rationalization** undergirded **not only slavery**, but also **later forms of systemic inequality including segregation, discriminatory law, and economic marginalization,** which scholars such as *Nell Irvin Painter* argue were

24

global in their reach - *"Ideas about black inferiority, rooted in a selective reading of scripture and amplified through science and social policy, shaped empires as much as nations"* (Painter 411).

The pseudo-scientific exploitation of this narrative continued well into the 20th century. Works such as *The Bell Curve* and others attempted to link intelligence to race, and drew upon assumptions *(already encoded)* in centuries of racialized biblical interpretation. By conflating **skin color** with moral, intellectual, and cultural worth, these frameworks falsely suggested that *people with darker skin—regardless of nationality, ethnicity, or culture—were inherently inferior to whites (Herrnstein and Murray 22).* I found it profoundly disturbing that a story meant to communicate the post-Flood relationships of Noah's sons had been weaponized into a global ideology of racial hierarchy affecting millions of lives and shaping entire societies.

This realization prompted reflection on the ethical responsibility of scholarship and faith. As James Cone notes in *The Cross and the Lynching Tree*, when religious narratives are manipulated to justify oppression, scripture becomes complicit in injustice: *"The God of the oppressed is not the God of those who oppress"* (Cone 35). The curse of Ham is not merely a historical artifact; it exemplifies the ways in which sacred texts can be distorted to legitimize domination by embedding racial prejudice into law, education, and culture.

Discovering this history also sharpened my awareness of systemic racism as a lived reality. It is not only expressed in violence but encoded into policies, social norms, and even theological interpretations. **The color of one's skin, the shape of one's features, the lineage one inherits—these became, in the minds of many, markers of divine favor or curse -** *a belief system that justified oppression across centuries and continents.* Recognizing this, I came to see that **confronting racism requires attention to both structural power and the ideological tools**—including *religious texts that have historically sustained it.*

Japheth's Spiritual Inclusion in the New Covenant

It is noteworthy—*and profoundly hopeful*—to acknowledge that, even though Jesus is not biologically descended from Japheth, Japheth's descendants are nonetheless spiritually included in the blessings of the Messiah through the New Covenant. In Genesis 9:26–27, Noah proclaims, *"Blessed be the Lord, the God of Shem! May God enlarge Japheth, and may he dwell in the tents of Shem"* (NIV). While the genealogical line of Jesus flows exclusively through Shem, the covenantal promises embedded in God's blessing extend beyond ethnic boundaries.

The New Testament reveals the fulfillment of this prophetic vision in "Gentiles" historically associated with the descendants of Japheth. They are brought into covenantal relationship with God through Christ. In Acts 10, Cornelius *(Italian)* - a Roman centurion - receives the Holy Spirit, marking a pivotal moment in the early Church. **God's salvation is not limited to the descendants of Shem or Israel but is offered to all nations** (Acts 10:44–48). Similarly, Paul emphasizes in Ephesians 2:11–19 that Gentiles—previously considered outsiders—are now "brought near" through Christ, reconciled to God and to one another, creating a unified body of believers irrespective of ethnic lineage. This spiritual inclusion demonstrates a profound theological truth - the covenant blessings of Shem, initially promised through Abraham and David - expand in Christ to encompass all peoples, fulfilling Noah's prophecy in a deeper, spiritual sense. Theologian *N.T. Wrigh*t observes that the mission of Jesus consistently transcends ethnic, cultural, and national boundaries, showing that God's plan is both particular and universal - *"God's people are not defined by birth alone, but by participation in the new covenant inaugurated in Christ"* (Wright 214).

Furthermore, this interpretation challenges historical misappropriations of scripture, as the **Hamitic Hypothesis** or racialized readings that sought *(and seek)* to elevate one ethnic group over another. By including Gentiles in the blessings of Shem, the New Covenant undermines racial and ethnic hierarchies, emphasizing faith and covenantal obedience over ancestry (Keller 102). Japheth's descendants, along with all peoples historically marginalized or misrepresented, are spiritually welcomed into God's kingdom, demonstrating that covenantal promises are not constrained by skin color or genealogy but are realized in Christ.

For me, this insight bridges scripture, personal faith, and social conscience. While Jesus' genealogical line is biologically through Shem, the gospel affirms that Japheth and all peoples—regardless of ethnicity, race, or historical oppression—can participate in God's covenant blessings. Noah's prophecy that Japheth would "dwell in the tents of Shem" finds its fulfillment not in racial supremacy but in spiritual communion, inclusion, and the radical egalitarianism of the Kingdom of God. This understanding reframes biblical ancestry as a spiritual reality rather than a tool of oppression, offering a *counter-narrative to centuries of racialized interpretations* and reminding us that divine blessing flows across all boundaries.

The Genealogy of Grace: Redemption Across Race and Nation

I strongly believe the Lord revealed this to me for a 21st-century reason - to help me and the citizens of the Kingdom of God, embrace a kingdom theology in a living and transformative way. Over the years, I have wrestled with race—personally, socially, and theologically. From the subtle humiliations I witnessed in my childhood - like Mr. Gross, the "debit man" - to the systemic structures of exclusion I encountered as a student at Milton Hershey School. I came to understand that human hierarchies—*racial, social, and economic*—have long distorted the divine vision. And yet, as I studied the scriptures, I began to see God's Kingdom emerging not as a reflection of human prejudice, but as a radical reversal of it, and I am convinced that no human system can ever overcome this demonically inspired distortion and global evil. Only the living reality of God's kingdom has the power to dismantle it.

27

Noah's prophecy in Genesis 9:25–27 had always troubled me, and I never actually knew why. I know, now, that it was not so much the pronouncement over Canaan to Ham that troubled me, but the distortion and the Hamitic Hypothesis that I have struggled with most of my life.

"Cursed be Canaan; a servant of servants shall he be to his brothers. Blessed be the Lord, the God of Shem... May God enlarge Japheth, and let him dwell in the tents of Shem, and let Canaan be his servant."

For centuries, this passage was exploited to justify slavery, colonization, and systemic oppression. The alleged **curse of Ham**—through Canaan—was *used to rationalize the subjugation of African peoples,* while the **blessings to Shem and Japheth** were *misread as divine endorsements of European (white) dominance.* Scholars like *Geraldine Heng and Nell Irvin Painter* have shown how these misinterpretations shaped entire societies, embedding racial hierarchies into law, commerce, and culture (Heng 105; Painter 411).

The God of the Kingdom never intended the story to end there. In the genealogy of Jesus, we see a divine subversion of human hierarchy. **Rahab,** a Canaanite woman, is *included in the lineage of the Messiah* (Matthew 1:5). Through her faith, the *line of Ham—once considered cursed—is grafted into God's covenant.* Ruth, a Moabite outsider, likewise demonstrates that God's inclusion transcends ethnic boundaries. Alongside them flows the line of Abraham and David, representing Shem, through which the Messianic covenant is fulfilled. Japheth, meanwhile, is included spiritually, because Gentiles are welcomed into the Kingdom through Christ, fulfilling Noah's prophecy that Japheth would "dwell in the tents of Shem" (Genesis 9:27; Acts 10:44–48; Ephesians 2:11–19).

This revelation revolutionized my understanding of Jesus' genealogy. It is far more than a historical record - it is a prophetic picture of the Kingdom of God - where grace, not ancestry, defines belonging. Paul articulates this principle in Galatians 3:28: *"There is neither Jew nor*

Greek, slave nor free, male nor female, for you are all one in Christ Jesus." **Shem provides the Messianic line**, ensuring continuity of covenant promises. **Ham is redeemed through Rahab. Japheth is brought in spiritually through the gospel's expansion to the Gentiles.** In this tapestry, *no lineage is excluded, no heritage is too marginalized, no outsider too distant to participate in the blessings of God.*

Kingdom theology teaches us that God's plan was global from the beginning. Rahab's inclusion signals that even the descendants of those historically oppressed—those deemed cursed by human interpretation— are invited into covenantal relationship. The Messiah came not just for one tribe or nation, but for all tribes, tongues, and peoples, fulfilling God's promise to Abraham that *"all nations of the earth will be blessed"* (Genesis 12:3). Scholars such as Amy-Jill Levine emphasize that the inclusion of figures like Rahab and Ruth illustrates God's purpose - faith, not ancestry, is the ultimate criterion for belonging (Levine 92). Similarly, James Cone reminds us that God consistently identifies with the marginalized, subverting systems of oppression and elevating the overlooked (Cone 35).

Reflecting on this in my own life, I see how the genealogy of Jesus is a living manifesto of divine justice and inclusion. The lessons I first glimpsed in my childhood—*the humiliation my father endured, the systemic inequalities around me, and the racial assumptions embedded in every facet of society*—are echoed and redeemed in the message of the Kingdom of God. The Messiah's lineage proclaims that what humans use to oppress, exclude, and diminish, God uses to redeem, incorporate, and bless. Rahab, Ruth, Abraham, David, and Jesus themselves collectively proclaim that no line, no race, no social or cultural status is beyond the reach of divine grace.

The message of the Kingdom of God reframes race not as a matter of hierarchy, but as a matter of "Kingdom inclusion." The Messiah's genealogy is not a family tree - it is a prophetic portrait of redemption - a divine blueprint for a world in which all are invited into one family under God. **Shem, Ham, and Japheth** - every descendant of Noah - is spiritually included in the Kingdom of God. This shows how the Kingdom is cosmic in scope, transformative in justice, and radical in grace. It is a Kingdom that challenges human systems of power, dismantles prejudice, demolishes discrimination, and calls all who follow Christ to participate in the work of reconciliation, justice, and inclusive love.

The Diabolical Strategy of Division and the Call of the Kingdom of God

Why have I, and so many of us, been so deeply troubled by race, prejudice, and racial discrimination? The answer is both spiritual and historical. From the very beginning, I think Satan's strategy has been one of division and corruption. In Genesis 3, humanity's first parents are tempted into disobedience - *severing their intimate union with God and ushering in the consequences of sin, alienation, and death.* In Genesis 4, Cain murders Abel - *demonstrating that the human family, created in God's image, is vulnerable to internal violence and jealousy.* By Genesis 11, at the Tower of Babel, humanity's ambition and pride result in linguistic, cultural, and geographic separation - *scattering the nations and creating the fertile soil for division that Satan has exploited for millennia.*

This spiritual and historical pattern illuminates why contemporary racism and prejudice are not merely social or political phenomena. They are manifestations of a deeper, spiritual disorder. I have wrestled with public discourse that reflects these enduring divisions, such as the statements of certain political figures who describe black and brown communities as inherently inferior or argue that civil rights initiatives undermine the supposed rights of white Americans. Theologically, this perspective is profoundly flawed. It echoes the same strategy of division, hierarchy, and fear that has perpetuated inequality since the earliest chapters of scripture.

I am deeply grieved, even as I acknowledge that individuals like Charlie Kirk are mortal human beings whose lives are complex, and I mourn the violence of his assassination. Yet, I also recognize that his statements exemplify the misuse of social, political, and historical narratives to justify privilege and deny others their God-given dignity. These narratives are false. No ethnic group is inherently superior, and no color of skin determines moral worth or intellectual capacity. The Kingdom of God, as proclaimed in Galatians 3:28, shatters all such hierarchies: *"There is neither Jew nor Greek, slave nor free, male nor female, for you are all one in Christ Jesus."* The gospel affirms that all human beings are created in God's image and are equally heirs of God's covenantal promises.

Historically, these theological truths have been central to movements for justice. Dr. Martin Luther King Jr. argued repeatedly that racial division is a moral, spiritual, and systemic issue rooted, not merely in ignorance, but in a rebellion against God's vision of the beloved community. As he stated in *Where Do We Go from Here: Chaos or Community? "Injustice anywhere is a threat to justice everywhere... Whatever affects one directly, affects all indirectly"* (King 78). King's prophetic theology insists that the struggle for racial equity is not merely political; it is a participation in God's Kingdom - *a divine mandate to restore shalom and repair the broken unity of the human family.*

Contemporary scholarship echoes this perspective. Miroslav Volf, in *Exclusion and Embrace*, notes that God's vision of humanity challenges all structures of exclusion and hierarchy: *"To be embraced is to be included in the community that mirrors God's own self-giving love, and exclusion is the antithesis of this divine vision"* (Volf 55). Similarly, James Cone observes that the gospel identifies God with the oppressed, not the oppressors, and insists that true discipleship demands solidarity with those whom the world marginalizes (Cone 35).

From this theological vantage point, notions that one racial or ethnic group is inherently entitled to privilege, whether through historical advantage, political power, or social systems, *are not simply errors of judgment.* They are manifestations of systemic evil and spiritual deception. The idea that Japheth, or *"white"* people, are inherently destined to dominate is not only historically false but theologically antithetical to the Kingdom of God. The gospel teaches that divine blessing is universally available, and that Jesus Christ came to redeem every tribe, tongue, and nation (Revelation 5:9).

This understanding transforms how we approach modern civil rights, equity initiatives, and social justice. Policies that seek to redress historical inequities—affirmative action, educational access, and reparative justice—are not threats to any group; they are expressions of God's Kingdom ethics in human society. They embody the principle that no one is outside of God's care, and that human systems must align themselves with divine justice to reflect the wholeness intended for all creation. In this sense, civil rights work is a "Kingdom mandate" - *a participation in the ongoing work of reconciliation and restoration that Christ inaugurated.*

Ultimately, my deep disturbance about racial injustice is rooted in the conviction that human division is a spiritual problem as well as a social one. Christ's Kingdom offers a radical alternative. In this Kingdom, no person is inherently inferior. No ethnic, cultural, or racial identity is a justification for exclusion, because all human beings are called to live in covenantal unity under the Messiah. To embrace this truth is to resist the diabolical schemes of division, honor God's image in every person, and work tirelessly toward a world where justice, inclusion, and love reign— exactly as Dr. Martin Luther King Jr. envisioned it.

A Narrative of Japheth and the Origins of "White" Identity

Long ago, after the flood, the sons of Noah spread across the earth. Shem, Ham, and Japheth carried the future of humanity in their families. The book of Genesis preserves their names in what is called the **Table of Nations** (Genesis 10) - a map of how tribes and peoples came to fill the world. Japheth, the eldest, was given a unique word of blessing. Noah said, "May God enlarge Japheth, and may he dwell in the tents of Shem" (Genesis 9:27). His destiny was to be enlarged — stretched outward into new lands, broad horizons, and distant coasts. But his enlargement was never meant to be a thing of pride or domination. It was meant to be coupled with humility. He would find his blessing, not in himself, but by dwelling in Shem's tents and receiving the covenant blessings that God would one day pour out through Israel and, ultimately, through Christ.

From Japheth's sons came many of the nations that we now recognize as the Indo-European (white) peoples. Gomer's children became the Cimmerians and the Celts - the ancestors of tribes who spread into what is now Europe. Magog's line became the Scythians, dwelling north of the Black Sea. Madai fathered the Medes of Persia. Javan gave rise to the Greeks - the Ionians of history and philosophy. Tubal and Meshech settled in Asia Minor, with echoes of their names still lingering in ancient place-names tied to Russia and Turkey, and Tiras was linked to the Thracians - a seafaring people of southeastern Europe.

Their children spread out along the coasts and into the continent — westward toward Spain, northward into Europe, and eastward into Persia. Over time, Japheth's descendants became Greeks and Romans, Celts and Germans, Slavs and Persians — the great Indo-European family of (white) nations.

But something happened much later in history. As the world entered the age of exploration and empire, Europeans (white people) began to think of themselves in a new way. They were no longer simply English,

33

French, German, or Spanish, but they began to call themselves "white." This word — "white" — does not appear in Scripture as an ethnic category. It was not a name given by God. It was **a human invention, born in the 17th and 18th centuries** as European powers conquered, colonized, and enslaved other peoples. By calling themselves "white," they drew a sharp line between themselves and others — "black, brown, red, and yellow." In doing so, they created not just categories but hierarchies.

This was the birth of racial supremacy. The enlargement that God had given Japheth — the ability to spread far, to sail seas, to build empires — was **twisted into a tool of domination.** Instead of dwelling in Shem's tents, many of Japheth's children sought to replace Shem, to act as if they themselves were the bearers of covenant blessing. Instead of honoring Ham's redemption, they reinforced a false curse, enslaving Ham's children for generations.

Supremacy was not Japheth's destiny. It was Satan's distortion - turning blessing into pride, and enlargement into empire. Yet, God's Word reminds us that this is not the final story. The nations — Shem, Ham, and Japheth together — are called into one family in Christ. Paul declares that in Jesus there is no Jew or Greek, slave or free, male or female (Galatians 3:28). The book of Revelation gives us the picture of the end of history - people from every tribe and tongue and nation standing before the throne, worshiping the Lamb (Revelation 7:9).

This is the hope for Japheth's children, and indeed for all peoples. The call is not to cling to "whiteness," nor to supremacy, but to humility — to dwell in the tents of Shem, to receive blessing through Jesus the Messiah and to walk alongside Ham and Shem as brothers, not rivals.

The story of Japheth's descendants is, in one sense, the story of Europe and the origins of "white" ethnicity. But it is also a story of warning — how easily blessing can be distorted by pride. It is, finally, a story of redemption — how God gathers back the nations, not under banners of race or empire, but under the cross of Christ.

Genesis 9:27 - Noah's Perceived Blessing and the Hamitic Hypothesis:

"May God enlarge Japheth, and let him dwell in the tents of Shem, and let Canaan be his servant."

The further exploitation of this scriptural reference spawned what has been exploited as a prophetic role of Japheth and, invariably, a sense of superiority among white people in America and worldwide.

The Hamitic hypothesis was a racial theory popularized in the 19th and early 20th centuries and, now, completely discredited. It claimed that all significant achievements in Africa were the result of a supposed "Hamitic race" — thought to be a branch of the Caucasian race — migrating into Africa and bringing civilization, technology, and governance. According to this view, sub-Saharan Africans (often labeled "Negroid" in the racist language of the time) were seen as incapable of developing advanced societies on their own.

The so-called Hamitic Hypothesis distorted biblical references to Noah's sons to argue that the descendants of Ham were responsible for Africa's great civilizations. According to this view, achievements in places like Egypt, Ethiopia, Great Zimbabwe, and Rwanda were not the work of indigenous sub-Saharan Africans but of supposed 'Hamites' from North and East Africa. This theory was used to diminish and erase the accomplishments of African peoples. In Rwanda, colonial authorities extended this into the so-called 'Hamitic myth,' portraying the Tutsi as a superior race with foreign (Hamitic) origins in contrast to the Hutu—an idea that later fueled ethnic divisions and contributed to the Rwandan genocide.[^1] Modern anthropology, archaeology, linguistics, and genetics have thoroughly discredited this hypothesis, recognizing it as a racist, Eurocentric (white) construct designed to legitimize colonial domination and white supremacy.[^2] In contrast, the biblical record presents Japheth's descendants as spreading widely across the earth, later associated with vast and influential empires such as Greece, Rome, Persia, and eventually the European kingdoms.[^3]

The **Hamitic hypothesis** played a key role in providing a perceived biblical and pseudo-scientific justification for slavery in the Americas and the transatlantic slave trade. Based on the Bible's "curse of Ham" → "curse of Canaan," slaveholders and European (white) intellectuals misinterpreted the biblical story in Genesis 9:18–27 - where Noah curses Canaan (Ham's son) - to be "a servant of servants." Over time, this was twisted into the so-called **"Curse of Ham"** (even though the Bible never says Ham was cursed). Europeans and White Americans conflated Ham's descendants with all Africans (sub-Saharan), claiming that Black people were divinely destined to be slaves.

Link to the Hamitic Hypothesis

By the 18th and 19th centuries, *the Hamitic hypothesis expanded this biblical misreading into a racial theory.* It proposed that "true civilization" in Africa was brought by supposedly lighter-skinned, non-Black Hamites. Meanwhile, darker-skinned Africans were cast as the cursed, inferior branch of Ham's lineage and fit only for servitude. America justified slavery and the Slave Trade with a presumed religious justification – *arguing that slaveholding in America and Europe was not only permissible but ordained by God, since sub-Saharan Africans were allegedly descended from Ham.* They created an erroneous moral cover allowing Christian societies to reconcile slavery with their faith by framing it as fulfilling God's will, and they promoted a deceptive economic justification, believing *(and promoting the belief)* that Africans were *"naturally suited"* for hard labor in plantations, which made it easier to rationalize their forced transportation and exploitation in the Americas.

A demonic colonial ideology was created, affirming the Hamitic hypothesis and reinforcing the idea that Africans could not create "civilization" on their own, making this useful propaganda for both slavery and colonial domination.

Long-term Consequences

This interpretation normalized slavery for centuries and deeply shaped racial ideologies in America. Even after abolition, the Hamitic hypothesis fueled scientific racism, segregation, and colonial rule in sub-Saharan Africa.

The Hamitic hypothesis — *rooted in a misreading of scripture and racial pseudo-science* — was used to legitimize the enslavement of sub-Saharan Africans, making the transatlantic slave trade and slavery in the Americas appear both "natural" and "divinely sanctioned."

For me, there is plausibility in presuming that Satan may have emboldened an anger in the descendants of Japheth—Europeans and white people—based on the fact that they were not included, biologically, in the genealogy of Jesus. This, of course, is my opinion; however, I believe it can be considered as a deep theological observation worth exegetical consideration. Scripture brings out how Satan's strategy has always been to exploit pride, anger, and feelings of exclusion in order to create division and oppose God's redemptive plan. From Eden to Revelation, Satan's tactics consistently exploit human pride, inflame anger, and intensify alienation. In contrast, God's redemptive plan centers on humility (Philippians 2:5–8), forgiveness (Colossians 3:13), and reconciliation (2 Corinthians 5:18–19).

Satan Exploiting Pride

Genesis 3:4–6 – In the garden, the serpent appeals to Eve's desire to "be like God," twisting pride into disobedience.

Isaiah 14:12–15 – Often understood as describing the fall of a proud heavenly being who sought to exalt himself.

1 Timothy 3:6 – Warning that a new convert must not be made an overseer, "or he may become conceited and fall under the same judgment as the devil."

Satan Stirring Anger

Genesis 4:5–7 – Cain's anger is manipulated, leading him to murder Abel. God warns him, "sin is crouching at your door."

Ephesians 4:26–27 – Paul urges believers not to let anger give "the devil a foothold."

Job 1:9–11; 2:4–5 – Satan seeks to provoke Job's bitterness against God.

Satan Feeding Feelings of Exclusion & Division

Numbers 16:1–3 – Korah incites rebellion by appealing to feelings of exclusion from leadership.

John 8:44 – Jesus says the devil is "a liar and the father of lies," describing how deception drives division.

2 Corinthians 2:10–11 – Paul warns the church to forgive, "so that Satan might not outwit us. For we are not unaware of his schemes."

Ephesians 2:14–16 – Christ brings reconciliation, tearing down walls of hostility — the opposite of Satan's divisive aims.

Revelation 12:10 – Satan is "the accuser of our brothers and sisters," fostering alienation and mistrust.

The issue, however, is not that Europeans or white people as *(descendants of Japheth)* have, somehow, been cut off from God's covenantal promises; rather, the genealogies in Matthew 1 and Luke 3 trace Jesus' biological lineage through Shem and specifically through Abraham and David. That is how the Messianic covenant was established (Genesis 12:1–3; 2 Samuel 7:12–16). The fact that Japheth is not named directly in Jesus' genealogy is not an exclusion, but the outworking of God's covenant through Shem. The deeper truth is that, in Christ, Japheth's descendants are spiritually included.

Noah's prophecy in Genesis 9:27—"May God enlarge Japheth, and may he dwell in the tents of Shem"—finds its ultimate fulfillment in the New Covenant. The gospel makes it clear that all nations, whether descended from Shem, Ham, or Japheth, are welcomed into the Kingdom of God. Paul affirms this when he declares that Gentiles, once "separated from Christ and alienated from the commonwealth of Israel," have now been "brought near by the blood of Christ" (Ephesians 2:12–13).

The tragedy, is not biological exclusion but spiritual misapprehension. At times, descendants of Japheth failed to fully embrace the spiritual inclusion given through Christ. Instead, they allowed pride, jealousy, and the desire for superiority to corrupt their participation in God's Kingdom. Satan exploited these distortions and turned the blessing of inclusion into a posture of domination. Instead of rejoicing to "dwell in the tents of Shem," some sought to build their own empires and justify their behavior by twisting Scripture and inventing the so-called *"curse of Ham."*

The Kingdom of God, however, reveals a different way. The truth of the gospel is that there is "neither Jew nor Greek, slave nor free, male nor female, for you are all one in Christ Jesus" (Galatians 3:28). All three branches of Noah's family—*Shem, Ham, and Japheth*—are embraced in Christ, not through biology but through covenant grace. The Messiah's genealogy is not a statement of exclusion but a prophetic picture pointing to the day when people "from every tribe and language and people and nation" will be redeemed and gathered before the throne (Revelation 5:9).

What Satan intended for division, God has already redeemed in Christ. The gospel calls us to resist the lies of pride and exclusion and instead embrace the profound unity that Jesus Christ has accomplished. Our task as in the Kingdom of God, and as the Church, is to live into that reality— *demolishing walls of hostility, rejecting racial hierarchies, and proclaiming the truth that in Christ, every nation is welcome at the table of the Kingdom of God.*

Why This Matters

Why does this matter? Because when Scripture is misused and interpreted through faulty hermeneutics—particularly Noah's words in Genesis 9:25–27—it does not remain a harmless mistake. Such distortions produced what came to be called the 'Hamitic Hypothesis' and the 'curse of Ham.' These ideas were weaponized to justify slavery, colonialism, and racial hierarchies, leaving deep scars on global society. They shaped the theology and practice of the American evangelical church, gave fuel to strands of Christian nationalist ideology, and weakened the witness of the Body of Christ. And their influence has not disappeared; it lingers, even today.

This false interpretation claimed that the so-called "curse of Ham" condemned all African peoples to perpetual slavery. It was one of the most destructive theological distortions in history, and it was used to justify the transatlantic slave trade, the enslavement of millions of Africans in America, and a racial hierarchy that equated dark skin with inferiority.

As scholars have noted, the **Hamitic Hypothesis** was a product - *not of divine truth* - but of human sin. David M. Goldenberg observes that *"the curse of Ham was never about blackness until it became politically and economically useful to Europeans and Americans seeking to justify slavery"* (Goldenberg 171).

In other words, **what began as a specific biblical narrative about Canaan was twisted into a blanket condemnation of Africa itself.** It was weaponized to provide *"divine sanction"* for oppression.

This matters because that false theology still reverberates. It undergirded centuries of colonialism, segregation, and the racist pseudoscience that culminated in works like *The Bell Curve* (Herrnstein and Murray), arguing that people of African descent were innately less intelligent. From plantation sermons telling enslaved people that their bondage was God's will, to 19th-century explorers like David Livingstone describing Africa as the "dark continent" in need of European control, the Hamitic Hypothesis became a global rationale for domination (Sanders 98).

But it was never intended by God or part of his plan for human beings, because the truth of the gospel directly contradicts these lies. In fact, as we have seen in the genealogy of Jesus, God deliberately included Rahab, a Canaanite woman descended from Ham. Her faith not only redeemed her own life but wove her into the Messianic line *(Matthew 1:5)*. This is no accident. It is a divine reversal of the so-called curse, showing that the Kingdom of God reclaims every lineage, every family, and every skin tone.

The inclusion of Rahab *(Ham)*, Ruth *(a Gentile outsider - Japheth)* and the central covenantal line of Shem, demonstrates that God's plan has always been inclusive. Noah's prophecy that Japheth would dwell in the tents of Shem (Genesis 9:27) is fulfilled in Christ. As Gentiles, *often descendants of Japheth,* they are grafted into the covenant by faith (Romans 11:17–24). Thus, in Jesus' very genealogy, the false divisions Satan has exploited for centuries are prophetically undone.

This also matters for today because racism and colorism still plague the world. In South Africa *(formerly under apartheid)*, in the caste-like discrimination within the Caribbean, in the anti-Black bias across Latin America, and in the United States with ongoing struggles with racial inequity, the shadow of the Hamitic Hypothesis still lingers. Lighter skin is too often equated with privilege and darker hues with disadvantage, but in the Kingdom of God, these hierarchies are dismantled. As Paul declared, *"Christ is all, and in all"* (Colossians 3:11).

So why am I so deeply troubled by race, prejudice, and racial discrimination? Because they are not merely social problems. **They are theological distortions and satanic strategies designed to deny the**

very heart of the gospel—that *Jesus came to redeem all nations.* **The Church's task, then, is to proclaim and embody the truth that the curse narrative has been overturned.** Every lineage is redeemed. Every hue reflects the image of God and, in Christ, every tribe, tongue, and nation finds its true home.

The Prophetic Tension of Japheth and the White European

Japheth's descendants *(Europeans - white people and related nations)* were not the line through which the Messiah would come. The covenant line was chosen through Shem, culminating in Abraham, Israel, David, and Jesus (Genesis 12:1–3; Matthew 1:1–16). Genesis 9:27 prophesies Japheth's destiny - *"May God enlarge Japheth, and let him dwell in the tents of Shem, and let Canaan be his servant."* This means that Japheth's blessing comes through Shem and is not separated from him. Spiritually, Japheth's descendants must enter into God's covenant by grace, not by genealogy or conquest.

Satan hates God's covenant and the Messiah. When Japheth's descendants grew into powerful empires *(Greece, Rome, and later European kingdoms)*, Satan whispered two key lies: *1)* **pride and supremacy** – *"You don't need to dwell in Shem's tents. You are chosen on your own terms."* - fueling white supremacy, colonialism and nationalism where European nations tried to replace God's covenant people rather than join them in humility *(Rome destroying Jerusalem in 70 AD and later became the center of a distorted imperial version of Christianity*; and *2)* **anger and resentment** – *"You were excluded, so take what is rightfully yours by force."* - creating hostility toward Jews, Africans, and other groups of color, turning spiritual insecurity into violence and oppression *(anti-Semitism, slavery, systemic racism)*. This same deception mirrors Satan's strategy in Eden - *"Has God really said...?"* (Genesis 3:1) — questioning God's plan and stirring up rebellion.

Explaining Further the Hamitic Hypothesis: Why Europeans and Some White People Feel Superior

The Canaanites, *who descended from Canaan,* were not Black in the modern sense. They lived in areas where populations were more olive, or light-skinned, and similar to other Semitic and Mediterranean peoples. They were Phoenicians, Hittites, Amorites, and other Canaanites with a lighter complexion due to geography and intermarriage. They were not Sub-Saharan Africans with a darker complexion of skin. The misconception that Ham represented *"all black people"* came from colonial interpretations, and Ham was wrongly used to justify slavery. The **"Curse of Ham"** teaching, which incorrectly claimed all of Ham's descendants were cursed and black, biblically, was only on Canaan *(Ham's son)* and not Ham's entire lineage. Noah pronounced the curse, but God did not (Genesis 9:25–27).

Ham's Descendants

Son	Region Settled	
Cush	Ethiopia, Sudan, parts of Arabia Dark-skinned *(African)*	
Mizraim	Egypt, parts of North Africa Brown to Light brown	
Phut	Libya, North Africa Olive to dark brown	
Canaan	Israel, Lebanon, Syria Olive, lighter-skinned	

Hamites and Blackness

Not all those whom colonial writers labeled as "Hamites" were imagined as dark-skinned. The so-called *Hamitic Hypothesis* was not only a grotesque misreading of Scripture but also an ideological weapon, crafted in the service of racism, slavery, and colonial domination. **It was not biblical at all**—it was a pseudo-scientific distortion, cobbled together from 19th- and early 20th-century racial fantasies masquerading as anthropology and theology. At its core, the hypothesis denied African peoples their own history by asserting that any trace of civilization, innovation, or cultural achievement in Africa could not possibly be indigenous. Instead, it claimed such advances were introduced by a supposedly "superior," lighter-skinned race of foreign origin, fraudulently traced to Ham but recast as Caucasian. In this way, Europeans could argue that the pyramids, Ethiopia's dynasties, or East African kingdoms were not genuinely African at all, but the work of outsiders. Meanwhile, Black Africans were relegated to a caricatured status as "cursed" and inherently backward, fit only to be ruled. This fiction conveniently justified Europe's imperial mission: if Africans had no real history of their own, then conquest and domination could be cast as both natural and necessary. The **Hamitic Hypothesis** was, in truth, **not history but propaganda**—*an intellectual alibi for white supremacy dressed up as biblical exegesis and racial "science.* "The Hamitic Hypothesis twisted Genesis 9:25–27 — **Noah's curse on Canaan** — into something much broader than what Scripture specifically says: *"Cursed be Canaan; a servant of servants shall he be to his brothers."*

The theory was distorted. The actual scriptural claim and curse was on Canaan alone, not all of Ham's descendants. **The Bible never said Ham was cursed,** and race *(as a modern concept)* didn't exist in biblical times. The text is about family lineages and territories, not skin color.

The Distortion

European theologians and anthropologists claiming that Ham himself, descendants of Ham were marked by dark skin and, therefore, Black Africans were "destined for slavery" is false and evil. This teaching was especially popular in the Atlantic slave trade era to justify enslaving Africans.

Points of Contact Between Japheth & Ham

As Japhethite groups—understood in this interpretive framework as *European white peoples*—expanded and engaged in trade and cultural exchange with lighter-skinned Hamitic populations, significant interactions developed across the Mediterranean. The Phoenicians *(descended from Canaan)* maintained extensive commercial ties with the Greeks *(descended from Javan),* while the Egyptians *(Mizraim, a Hamitic lineage)* also conducted regular trade with Mediterranean nations. These maritime routes created a natural network linking Japhethite and lighter-skinned Hamitic societies. Over time, conquest and colonization enabled Japhethite nations to expand their military and political dominance, progressively subduing Hamitic peoples—most notably the Canaanite branch. The empires of Greece and Rome *(identified with Javan)* brought *Egypt, Carthage, and other Hamitic territories* under their control. Centuries later, modern European colonial powers—*England, France, Spain, and Portugal (viewed as modern Japhethite nations)*—extended this pattern through their domination of sub-Saharan Africa and the Caribbean. In this misinterpretive reading, such historical developments were seen as a direct outworking of the biblical motif of Canaan serving Japheth.

Spiritual Alignment

The prophecy of Japheth dwelling in the tents of Shem has a spiritual fulfillment: the covenant blessings that originated with Shem's line— Israel, fulfilled in Jesus and carried forward by the early Church—were eventually received by Japhethite peoples such as the Greeks, Romans, and later Europeans. In this sense, Japheth "entered Shem's tents" by sharing in the covenant through Christ. Yet what was meant as a sign of unity and reconciliation was twisted by sin into an ideology of domination. Instead of embracing the covenant as a gift of grace, Japhethite nations weaponized it to justify conquest and exploitation. This perversion reached its most grotesque form in the **Trans-Atlantic Slave Trade,** where Europeans (Japheth) enslaved millions of sub-Saharan Africans (associated with Ham), claiming divine right as their warrant. The Hamitic Hypothesis—an unbiblical fabrication—further entrenched this racial hierarchy, portraying Japheth as destined to rule and Ham as doomed to servitude. Colonialism intensified the distortion:

at the Berlin Conference of 1884–85, European powers carved Africa into territories for their own profit, drawing borders with complete disregard for the lives, histories, and sovereignties of indigenous peoples. These acts were not the fulfillment of God's promise but the corruption of it—the fallen misuse of Japheth's enlargement, an abuse of Scripture to sanctify greed, slavery, and empire.

In Simple Terms

Ham's descendants of lighter skin built early civilizations. Japheth's descendants spread widely, eventually becoming the European and Western nations. At first, they traded and interacted normally then, over time, Japhethites conquered and enslaved the sub-Saharan Hamites, especially through colonization and the slave trade. Spiritually, Japheth was supposed to *share in Shem's covenant blessings* through Christ, but sin twisted this into racial hierarchies and oppression. In the Kingdom, Jesus restores all three lines, making a new humanity where Shem, Ham, and Japheth are united as sons and daughters of God.

Where the biblical misreadings and the rise of modern racial theories meet is in the European's claims of white superiority by combining the misinterpretations of Noah's prophecy with Enlightenment-era racial science and colonial interests.

Twisting Noah's Prophecy

By twisting and misinterpreting Genesis 9, some constructed a false biblical justification: that Black Africans were "cursed" and destined for servitude, while Europeans were "blessed" and divinely appointed as rulers. This distortion expanded the curse far beyond its biblical scope, wrongly applying it to all descendants of Ham and equating Ham himself with both North African and sub-Saharan peoples. Europeans, identifying themselves as descendants of Japheth, then portrayed their global expansion as the fulfillment of being "enlarged" and ordained to dominate. Yet Scripture is clear that only Canaan, Ham's son, was named in the curse—not Ham, nor his other descendants.

The "Curse of Ham" and Justifying Slavery

During the transatlantic slave trade (1500s–1800s), pro-slavery theologians claimed sub-Saharan Africans were naturally slaves because of Ham's curse. This became a moral shield for Christian nations that wanted to profit from slavery but still call themselves *"godly."*

The Hamitic Hypothesis

In the 19th century, many European scholars advanced the claim that Africa's great civilizations—such as Egypt, Ethiopia, and Great Zimbabwe—could not have been built by sub-Saharan Black Africans. Instead, they attributed these achievements to so-called "Hamitic Caucasians" from northern or eastern Africa. This theory implied that sub-Saharan Africans were inherently incapable of creating advanced societies. Thus, whenever Europeans encountered evidence of high culture, architecture, or political organization in Africa, they credited it to a supposedly lighter-skinned, foreign-originating group rather than to the indigenous peoples themselves.

The Enlightenment and the "Science of Race"

European theorists such as Carl Linnaeus and Johann Blumenbach developed early racial classifications that divided humanity into distinct "races." In their hierarchies, Caucasians (Europeans) were placed at the top as the most "beautiful, rational, and civilized." By contrast, Africans were ranked at the bottom and described as "primitive" or "closer to animals." Within this scheme, a distinction was drawn between Upper/North Africans (Egyptians, Berbers, Ethiopians), who were sometimes recast as "Hamites" and viewed as closer to Caucasians, and Sub-Saharan Africans, who were regarded as the "truest" Africans and depicted as inherently backward. This pseudoscience, when merged with distorted interpretations of the Bible, gave Europeans both a theological and a so-called "scientific" rationale for enslavement, colonialism, and racial domination.

Colonialism & Global Power

By the 1800s, European nations—identified in this framework as descendants of Japheth—controlled vast areas of the globe. Their military, technological, and economic dominance was portrayed as "proof" of racial superiority. Missionaries, scholars, and political leaders presented colonization as a divinely sanctioned mission: to bring "civilization" and Christianity to the so-called "cursed" descendants of Ham. Within this narrative, **Upper Africans**—such as Egyptians, Berbers, and Ethiopians—were often depicted as relatively advanced or partially aligned with European civilization, whereas **Sub-Saharan Africans** were portrayed as entirely backward and in need of European guidance. Christianity, intertwined with these racialized assumptions, was used instrumentally: it provided a moral and theological rationale for conquest, the Trans-Atlantic Slave Trade, and colonial exploitation, presenting domination as a divine duty rather than an act of economic or political self-interest.

The Core Logic of White Superiority

Bible distortion – Ham perceived as Africa, cursed and destined for servitude.

Pseudoscience – Europeans deemed naturally superior race.

History/power – European global dominance interpreted as destiny fulfilled.

Together, these ideas hardened into white supremacy — a system where Europeans believed they were ordained (by God and by "science") to rule over others. Europeans claimed white superiority by merging a twisted reading of Noah's prophecy (Japheth ruling, Ham cursed) with racial pseudoscience and their own colonial dominance. This framework justified slavery, colonialism, and systemic racism as "natural" and "divinely ordered," even though the Bible itself never teaches racial hierarchy.

The Early Church, Biblical Interpretation, Greco-Roman intellectual Frameworks and Japhethite Notions of Superiority

The early Church was profoundly influenced by both biblical interpretation and Greco-Roman intellectual traditions. Ideas of Japhethite superiority—derived from the "Table of Nations" in Genesis 10, which traces humanity to Noah's sons Shem, Ham, and Japheth—were occasionally invoked in ways that reinforced social and cultural hierarchies. The biblical foundation for this notion comes from Genesis 9 and the post-Flood account in which Noah's sons are presented as the progenitors of all humanity. In Genesis 9:27, Noah says, "May God enlarge Japheth, and let him dwell in the tents of Shem." Later interpretive traditions often read this verse as a prophecy of Japheth's expansion and influence, at times implying dominance even over Shem and Ham.

Jewish Interpretive Traditions *(Pre-Christian)*

Some Second Temple Jewish texts and later rabbinic writings associated Japheth with Greeks and other Indo-European peoples, often understood as lighter-skinned or "white." Japheth was frequently linked with attributes such as beauty, culture, and intellectual refinement. In contrast, Ham was sometimes associated with African peoples, with distinctions drawn between **Upper Africans**—including Egyptians, Berbers, and Ethiopians, often viewed as more advanced—and **Sub-Saharan Africans**, who were depicted as less developed. Shem was consistently connected with Israel and the Hebrew people. These associations created a framework in which Japhethite peoples were idealized for their perceived refinement, Hamitic peoples were hierarchically categorized, and Shem's line was defined by covenantal and spiritual significance.

Early Christian Reception

Early Christian writers and Church Fathers, including Augustine, Jerome, and Eusebius, developed ethnographic interpretations of Genesis 10—the "Table of Nations"—to account for the origins and characteristics of different peoples. Genesis 10 traces humanity to Noah's sons Shem, Ham, and Japheth, and these lineages became a framework for understanding cultural, spiritual, and political distinctions. **Japheth's descendants** were associated with Europeans and other Indo-European peoples, including Greeks, Romans, and later northern tribes, and were often linked to expansion, empire-building, and intellectual or cultural dominance—qualities exemplified in Greco-Roman civilization. **Shem's descendants** were tied to Israel and the Hebrew peoples, emphasizing spiritual priority and covenantal blessing, a line culminating in Judaism and Christianity. **Ham's descendants** were associated with African and parts of Near Eastern populations, with commentators distinguishing between **Upper Africans**—such as Egyptians, Berbers, and Ethiopians, seen as relatively advanced—and **Sub-Saharan Africans**, often portrayed as less developed.

While some Church Fathers interpreted the phrase "dwelling in the tents of Shem" spiritually—indicating that Gentiles (Japhethites) could share in the blessings of Israel through Christ—there was also an implicit hierarchical reading. Japheth became associated with worldly expansion and intellectual achievement, Shem with spiritual priority, and Ham with marginalization. Tragically, this hierarchical framing laid a foundation for later racialist misinterpretations in medieval and modern periods, which distorted these biblical categories to justify conquest, slavery, and systemic subordination.

Superiority Narratives

The idea of Japhethite superiority emerged when Christian thinkers aligned Roman/Greek cultural dominance with Japheth's "enlargement" and the conversion of Gentiles as Japheth "dwelling in Shem's tents." This framework let the church see the Roman/European mission as providential and legitimate. It also created space for subtle hierarchies between ethnic groups—though in the early church, it was more cultural/intellectual than racial in a modern sense.

Legacy

In the medieval period, Japheth increasingly became associated with Europe, Shem with Asia, and Ham with Africa. Within this framework, **Upper Africans**—including Egyptians, Berbers, and Ethiopians—were sometimes viewed as more advanced or culturally aligned, while **Sub-Saharan Africans** were depicted as less developed. This mapping reinforced a worldview in which Japheth/Europe was seen as destined for global expansion and political dominance. Although the early Church did not explicitly preach racial superiority, its emphasis on Japhethite expansion as providential—linked to Greco-Roman cultural dominance and the Christian mission—created interpretive foundations that later theological and ideological traditions would exploit to justify European supremacy, colonialism, and the subjugation of African peoples.

What a Biblical Ethnography, Theology and Empire Politics Fused

Rome emerged as the imperial center for what came to be perceived as Japhethite superiority in the early Church through a combination of scriptural interpretation, providential history, and political circumstance. The Church interpreted passages from Genesis 10—particularly the Table of Nations and the blessing of Japheth—as foreshadowing the expansion and influence of Japheth's descendants. At the same time, the historical rise of Rome as the dominant political and military power in the Mediterranean reinforced the notion that European-descended peoples were naturally suited for governance, culture, and intellectual leadership. The Christianization of the empire under Constantine and his successors further fused religious authority with political and cultural power, portraying Rome not only as the seat of earthly empire but also as the vehicle through which divine providence extended Japhethic influence. This convergence of theology, scripture, and imperial reality helped establish a worldview in which Europe—and by extension, Japhethite peoples—were seen as both spiritually and materially destined to lead, a framework that would later inform medieval and modern interpretations of European superiority.

After the Flood, Noah's three sons—Shem, Ham, and Japheth—became the progenitors of the nations of the earth. Genesis 10 traces the spread of their descendants across the world, establishing the foundations of human diversity. **Japheth's descendants**—including Gomer, Magog, Madai, Javan, Tubal, Meshech, and Tiras—moved into the coastlands and distant territories, later associated with Greeks, Romans, and other Indo-European peoples. **Ham's descendants**—Cush, Mizraim, Put, and Canaan—settled in Africa and parts of the Near East, with some, like the Egyptians and Ethiopians, emerging as advanced civilizations, while others farther south were portrayed in later interpretations as less developed. **Shem's descendants**—Elam, Asshur, Arphaxad, Lud, and Aram—remained primarily in the Near East, preserving the line from which Israel would emerge.

The chapter concludes by emphasizing that all these families and nations were distributed according to their territories, each with its own language and culture. While Genesis 10 presents a genealogical and geographical record, later interpreters layered it with symbolic and hierarchical meanings: Japheth was associated with expansion, culture, and influence; Shem with spiritual inheritance and covenant; and Ham— particularly Canaan—became, in some readings, linked to marginalization. This narrative of human dispersal laid the foundation for both early theological reflection and, tragically, later misuses of the text in racialized and colonial ideologies.

Theological Groundwork - *Japheth Enlarged*

Genesis 9:27—"May God enlarge Japheth, and let him dwell in the tents of Shem"—was originally a statement about the blessing and expansion of Noah's descendants. Early interpreters saw it as indicating that Japheth's line would grow and spread, both territorially and culturally, and that Gentiles could share in the covenantal blessings of Israel through Christ. In this sense, the verse was about inclusion, spiritual participation, and the universality of God's plan, not about racial hierarchy or dominance.

Over time, however, this passage was co-opted to justify social and political hierarchies. Within the ethnographic framework of Genesis 10, Japheth's descendants—identified with Greeks, Romans, and later Europeans—were portrayed as culturally refined and expansionist. Shem's descendants retained spiritual primacy, while Ham's descendants—particularly Sub-Saharan Africans—were marginalized or depicted as inherently backward. This reinterpretation transformed a text of blessing and inclusion into a pseudo-theological rationale for European supremacy, colonial conquest, and the subjugation of African peoples. Rome, and later European empires, were cast as divinely appointed instruments of Japhethite enlargement, a distortion that conflated providence with empire-building, and inclusion through Christ with racialized domination.

Rome as the Fulfillment of Prophecy

Eusebius of Caesarea (early 4th c.), in his Ecclesiastical History and Chronicle, framed Rome as the climax of world empires, prepared by God to host Christianity. Rome was cast as the universal empire that gathered all nations (Japheth's expansion) and now provided a stage for the Gospel to spread. Thus, Rome's rule wasn't just political - it was sacralized within salvation history.

From Jerusalem to Rome

Originally, Jerusalem represented the theological and covenantal "center," rooted in Shem's heritage. However, following the destruction of the Temple in 70 CE and the expansion of Christianity beyond Judea, religious and moral authority gradually shifted westward. Rome—where key figures such as Peter and Paul were martyred—came to be re-envisioned as a "new Jerusalem," the seat of apostolic authority and spiritual governance. Within the ethnographic framework of Genesis 10, this development aligned with the concept of Japheth's enlargement: Japhethite peoples, associated with expansion, culture, and governance, were now positioned at the center of both political and spiritual life. Rome thus became a symbolic and practical capital, embodying the convergence of Japhethite influence and the inclusive reach of God's covenant through Christ.

Imperial Christianity

Constantine's conversion (early 4th c.) bound the Church and empire together. The empire's universality was read as part of God's plan. Rome would equal Japheth's global dominion and see it as baptized into Christ. The Church Fathers began to see Rome not just as a secular empire but as the Christian empire, legitimizing both papal and imperial authority.

Rome as Arbiter of Hierarchy

Once Rome became the center of both Church and empire, Japhethite ideology hardened into a worldview of hierarchical dominance. **Europe (Japheth)** was portrayed as destined for expansion, governance, and cultural leadership. **Asia (Shem)**, while the original bearer of revelation, was subordinated under the political and spiritual authority of Rome. **Africa (Ham)** was marginalized, with later interpretations drawing a sharp distinction between **Upper Africans**—including *Egyptians, Berbers, and Ethiopians,* sometimes credited with limited cultural achievements—and **Sub-Saharan Africans**, who were depicted as backward, servile, or "cursed." These ethnographic distortions transformed a genealogical text into a pseudo-theological hierarchy.

Rome, in this framework, became both the spiritual and political embodiment of Japheth's enlargement: *expanded, ruling, yet "dwelling in the tents of Shem" through Christianity as the fulfillment of Judaism.* It was reimagined as a providential empire, a *"new Jerusalem"* that replaced Shem's original center, and a hub for the universal Christian mission. *Over time, this framework was exploited to justify European domination, cultural erasure, and, eventually, racialized ideologies that portrayed sub-Saharan Africans as inherently inferior.* What began as an interpretive reading of Genesis 10 and 9 was transformed into a moral and theological alibi for conquest, colonialism, and the systemic oppression of African peoples.

How this Rome-centered Japhethic Ideology Evolved in the Middle Ages: *Crusading and Colonial Justifications*

The trajectory from early church Japhethic ideology to medieval and early modern imperialism is fascinating, because it shows how biblical interpretation, church authority and geopolitics reinforced each other over centuries.

Late Antiquity (4th–6th c.)

Rome became the imperial center of Christendom, and Japhethic expansion was still linked to European dominion. **Isidore of Seville** (7th c.) codified the *Table of Nations* in *Etymologiae* - **Europe** is Japheth and white. **Asia is** Shem, and **Africa** is Ham and black. This becomes a standard ethnographic map for medieval Europe, and Japheth's *"superiority"* is deemed *cultural, territorial, and spiritual*—Europeans are heirs to Rome's universalizing mission.

High Middle Ages (11th–13th c.)

The ideology became mobilized for crusading. Papal decrees framed Europe *(Japheth)* **as the defender and spreader of Christendom,** and Shem's lands *(Middle East)* were spiritually central but often **politically dominated by Japhethite knights and kings.** Ham's descendants *(Africa)* were increasingly coded as inferior and pagan, rationalizing their conquest and subjugation. The **Roman church** *(papacy)* cast itself as **arbiter of God's providential plan, linking spiritual and temporal authority.**

Late Middle Ages (14th–15th c.)

Exploration and early colonialism began, and **biblical Japhethite ideology justified European expansion.** Europe *(Japheth)* was destined to *"enlarge,"* conquer, and civilize. **Africa and Asia were earmarked as regions for conversion and control.** *Chronicles, maps, and sermons* explicitly used Genesis 9–10 to naturalize European/white dominance, and Rome's authority *(papacy)* was central in granting legitimacy—e.g., papal bulls granting lands in **the New World.**

Early Modern Period (16th–18th c.)

Japhethic ideology was now fully **racialized** in some texts. **Ham's "curse" is used to justify slavery in Africa,** and Shem remains spiritually central *(Middle East, Semitic peoples)* as Europe/Rome/Japheth exercises **cultural, political, and military dominion.** *The Church and State work together to provide a religio-political narrative of European superiority that is rooted in scriptural interpretation.*

The Key Mechanisms for Rome-Centered Japhethic Ideology

Scriptural exegesis based on Genesis 9–10 as providential justification, and a universal empire as Rome's historical expansion equated with Japheth's "enlargement." **The Church** was recognized as an authority, as **the papacy mediated divine mandates for conquest and civilization.** Ethnographic codification recognized *Europe as Japheth, Africa as Ham, and Asia as Shem,* and a cultural ideology, based on European dominance, was recognized as the fulfillment of God's plan.

Rome started out as the imperial hub in early Christianity due to providential readings of Genesis. By the Middle Ages, it became the **spiritual and political nerve center of Japhethic/European (white) expansion.** This ideology was then mobilized for crusading, exploration, and colonialism, linking the biblical narrative of Genesis 9 to European claims of cultural and territorial superiority.

The Vatican and Catholicism

The Vatican and Catholicism did not merely *inherit* Japhethic-European ideology; they became its chief architects and global enforcers. Far from passive, the papacy actively *affirmed and sanctified* European (white) supremacy through doctrine, decrees, and papal bulls that authorized conquest, enslavement, and expansion. The so-called "spiritual authority" of Rome wrapped itself around the political ambitions of Europe, making colonization not only permissible but a divinely sanctioned duty.

The **"Doctrine of Discovery"** in the 15th century is a prime example. Issued in papal bulls such as *Dum Diversas* (1452), *Romanus Pontifex* (1455), and *Inter Caetera* (1493), the Vatican explicitly gave Christian monarchs the right to seize lands, enslave non-Christians, and treat non-European peoples as subhuman obstacles to be subdued. This was Japhethic enlargement weaponized—Rome baptizing European greed and conquest as the unfolding of divine prophecy. What was originally a biblical vision of covenantal inclusion ("dwelling in the tents of Shem") was twisted into a justification for dominion, subjugation, and racial hierarchy.

The Roman Church proclaimed itself the *new Jerusalem*, yet in practice, it replaced Shem's covenantal center with Japheth's imperial power. Its theology fused with empire to create a machinery of domination that stretched from the Americas to Africa and Asia. Even within Africa, distinctions were reinforced: **Upper Africans** (Egyptians, Berbers, Ethiopians) were sometimes portrayed as *"civilizable"* because of their ancient ties to Christianity, while **Sub-Saharan Africans** were cast as perpetually *"cursed"* and fit for enslavement. Thus, **the Vatican gave theological cover to the Trans-Atlantic Slave Trade, colonial partition, and the cultural erasure of entire peoples.**

This was not providence—it was perversion. It was not prophecy fulfilled, but prophecy distorted. The Vatican enthroned Japhethic superiority as divine destiny, making the Church complicit in the blood of nations and in the global racial order that still scars the world. **Rome did not simply dwell in the tents of Shem; it looted them, renamed them, and claimed them as its own, turning covenant into conquest.**

The Vatican as Arbiter of Divine Providence

By the High Middle Ages, the papacy was no longer a mere shepherd of souls—it had enthroned itself as the universal monarch of Christendom. The Pope claimed to be God's vicar on earth, the mouthpiece of heaven, with authority to crown kings, divide lands, and dictate the destiny of nations. Rome fused theology with power and baptized empire itself.

This self-exaltation was bound to Japhethic-European ideology in two decisive ways. **First**, the papacy reinterpreted Genesis 9:27—"May

God enlarge Japheth, and let him dwell in the tents of Shem"—so that Europeans were cast as covenantal heirs through the Church. To "dwell in Shem's tents" no longer meant the inclusion of Gentiles into Israel's covenant through Christ; it was twisted into a theological charter for Europe's supremacy. **Second**, the Vatican assumed moral authority over conquest, blessing European expansion as the unfolding of divine prophecy. What was once a promise of covenantal fellowship became a mandate for dominion.

Out of this distortion came the so-called *Doctrine of Discovery*. Through papal bulls such as *Dum Diversas* (1452), *Romanus Pontifex* (1455), and *Inter Caetera* (1493), the Vatican gave Christian monarchs divine license to seize foreign lands, enslave non-Christians, and strip entire peoples of dignity and sovereignty. With one hand it held the cross, and with the other it wielded the sword. Europe's greed was clothed in holiness; colonization was baptized as providence.

Even Africa was divided within this ethnographic imagination. **Upper Africans**—Egyptians, Berbers, Ethiopians—were sometimes acknowledged as "civilizable" because of ancient ties to Christianity. **Sub-Saharan Africans**, however, were cast as the perpetual "cursed," fit for bondage, their labor and bodies reduced to commodities in the trans-Atlantic slave trade. This was Japheth's enlargement weaponized, sanctified, and globalized—Rome enthroning Europe as the ruler of nations and the arbiter of humanity itself.

This was not a covenant; it was corruption. Not prophecy fulfilled, but prophecy twisted into ideology. The papacy enthroned whiteness as divine destiny and became the theological architect of the modern empire. From the crowns of Spain and Portugal to the plantations of the Americas and the partition of Africa, the blood of nations testifies against this counterfeit gospel. Rome did not simply dwell in Shem's tents; it plundered them, claimed them, and declared them its own, replacing

God's vision of shared blessing with a global machinery of conquest and racial hierarchy.

Papal Bulls and Colonial Endorsements
Doctrine and documents gave concrete expression to Japhethic superiority:

The Dum Diversas (1452) where **Pope Nicholas V** authorized Portuguese kings to conquer and subjugate non-Christians.

The Romanus Pontifex (1455) extended Portugal's authority over African   territories.
The Inter Caetera (1493) where **Pope Alexander** VI divided the New World between Spain and Portugal.

These documents reflected the ideological map of Japheth (Europe and whites), Shem (the Middle East and Asians), and Ham (Africa and blacks). European expansion was gained by providential right, and non-Christian peoples became subjects of conversion or conquest.

Missionary Activities

When Protestant nations broke from Rome, they claimed to have thrown off the yoke of papal corruption. But in truth, they carried the same Japhethic ideology forward—stripped of the Pope, yet baptized in their own theologies. The crown of Europe's supremacy did not fall with the Vatican; it was simply rebranded in Geneva, London, Amsterdam, and eventually Boston.

Protestant missions became the new spearhead of the empire. The same *"dwelling in Shem's tents"* motif reappeared, but now under Protestant banners. England's Church of England, the Dutch Reformed Church, and later American Puritan and evangelical movements declared themselves heirs of the covenant, bringing the "light of the gospel" to the so-called "heathen" nations. Yet as with Rome, conversion was never only spiritual—it was tethered to political and cultural domination.

In Africa, Protestant missionaries reinforced the same racial distinctions: **Upper Africans** *(Ethiopians, Copts, North Africans)* were treated as "noble remnants" who might be integrated into a Christianized modernity, while **Sub-Saharan Africans** were cast as *"dark," "primitive," and in need of strict European guidance—or worse, as destined for perpetual servitude.* In the Americas, **Puritans and later evangelicals justified the dispossession and near extermination of Indigenous peoples as clearing the way for "God's chosen" European settlers**. In India and the Pacific, missionary schools imposed European norms, suppressing native cultures while claiming to uplift them.

Where the Vatican once issued papal bulls, **Protestant powers issued charters, treaties, and missionary societies**—*all cloaked in the same distorted theology of Japheth's enlargement.* The ***Doctrine of Discovery*** was not abandoned; it was absorbed into Protestant legal and colonial frameworks, providing justification for English expansion, Dutch trading empires, and eventually **American "Manifest Destiny."**

Thus, **Protestantism proved no antidote to Catholic imperial theology;** it was its continuation. **Both Rome and the Reformation baptized the same lie:** *that European domination was God's will, that Japheth was destined to enlarge by ruling, and that the peoples of Ham and Shem must be subordinated within his tents.* The difference was only in form—**papal bulls or Protestant manifestos**—but the spirit was the same.

This was not the kingdom of God—*it was the kingdom of men cloaked in God's name.* Whether Catholic or Protestant, Rome or Geneva, papal or Puritan, the machinery of conquest marched forward, carrying cross and cannon together. The gospel was chained to the empire, and Christ was invoked as the patron of colonizers. In this, Europe twisted covenant into conquest and turned the tents of Shem into the barracks of Japheth.

Theological Writings

Church scholars reinforced the erroneous and manipulative ideology, as Rome's role, as the universal church, meant that **Catholicism institutionalized Japhethic expansion and blended theology with geopolitics.**

Isidore of Seville codified Europe as Japheth (white).

Thomas Aquinas (and later scholastics) justified hierarchical social order, recognizing Europeans as "superior" by virtue of a divine plan.

Mechanisms of Affirmation

It was papal authority that granted spiritual and temporal legitimacy to European (white) rulers. The missionaries sanctioned it by justifying conquest and conversion as a divine mandate. An ethnographic theology reinforced Europe (Japheth, white) as culturally, politically, and spiritually superior, and codification in canon and civil law legislated papal bulls as they became legally binding instruments for European powers.

Catholicism and the Vatican affirmed Japhethic notions of superiority by linking Rome as spiritual center to Europe's political expansion, sanctioning conquest and conversion via papal authority, and embedding this hierarchy into theology, law, and missionary practice. The result was a fully institutionalized Japhethic worldview that guided Europe's medieval and early modern expansion.

Dum Diversas (1452) – Pope Nicholas V

The content authorized King Alfonso V of Portugal to "attack, conquer, and subjugate Saracens and pagans." The Japhethic link was that Europe (Portugal) Japheth destined to expand. Ham (Africa) and blacks were to be subjugated and defined as non-Christian peoples, while Shem (Middle East) would be partially Christianized, but still under European influence. The first formal papal endorsement of European conquest was seen as a divine mandate.

Romanus Pontifex (1455) – Pope Nicholas V

The content extended Portugal's rights over African territories and legitimized trade monopoly and slavery of non-Christians. It confirms Europe (Japheth, white) as divinely sanctioned to "enlarge" into foreign lands, and papal authority converted biblical typology into international law.

Inter Caetera (1493) – Pope Alexander VI

The content divided the "New World" between Spain and Portugal, and indigenous peoples were converted to Christianity. Spain and Portugal became recognized as Japheth/European and white, executing God's providential plan. The Indigenous Americas was often coded as Ham/blacks *(pagan/"cursed")* *and* subordinate to European/Japeth/white expansion. Institutionalized Japhethic/European and white hierarchy became a global phenomenon.

Catholic Missionary Doctrine

Franciscans, Jesuits, and Dominicans actively framed their work as a fulfillment of Japheth/European/ whites dwelling in Shem's tents according to Genesis 9:27, and Europe (Japheth) brought Christianity and civilization to Ham/"pagan" lands with a spiritual and cultural hierarchy reinforced through education, conversion, and governance.

Scholastic and Theological Reinforcement

Isidore of Seville codified Europe as white Japheth, Africa as black= Ham, and Asia as Shem/Israel.

Thomas Aquinas & other successors, justified these social and political hierarchies as being divinely ordained and Rome as center and through the papacy embodied Japhethic/white authority, guiding the expansion, sanctioning the exegetical interpretation of Genesis 9 and the hierarchy that went along with ot.

How It Worked into a Global Institutional System

Component	Role in Japhethic Ideology
Papal Bulls	*Legal and spiritual authorization for European expansion*
Missionaries	*Spiritual justification for conquest and "civilization"*
Theologians/Scholastics	*Codification of hierarchical worldview*
Rome/Vatican	*Central authority linking Japheth (Europe) to the divine plan*

Through papal authority, legal instruments, missionary activity, and theological scholarship, the Vatican turned Japhethic notions into an institutionalized framework: Europe (Japheth) as spiritually and politically dominant, Ham's descendants subordinated, and Shem's lands integrated into European Christian control. Rome was the central hub where ideology, law, and divine sanction converged.

The Protestant Focus of the Reformation

The Protestant Reformation focused on doctrinal, liturgical, and ecclesiastical reforms, and did not wish not to overturn the Eurocentric, Japhethic, white worldview that the Catholic Church had institutionalized.

Martin Luther, John Calvin, and other reformers aimed to establish Reform theology (e.g., justification by faith, sola scriptura) and correct perceived abuses in the Church (indulgences, papal authority, corruption). They wanted to restructure church governance, and an ethno-geopolitical ideology was not a primary target for them.

They were concerned with salvation, scripture, and church practice, and not with overturning the biblical ethnography linking Japheth/white to Europe. Early Protestants retained much of the inherited medieval worldview, and the understanding the Europe (Japheth, white) was culturally and spiritually dominant. To them, Africa and the Americas were coded as lands of paganism or Ham's descendants, and they accepted Rome and the historical papacy that sanctioned the expansion. However, they reinterpreted it through a Protestant lens— criticizing papal abuses without questioning the underlying Eurocentric worldview.

By the 16th century, Europeans were already globalizing Protestant nations *(England, the Netherlands, Scandinavia)* and entering into exploration and colonization. Missionaries were working in the Americas, Africa, and Asia and advancing the Japhethic logic that Europe was spiritually and culturally superior. Protestant reformers often endorsed this imperial and colonial expansion, and framed it as spreading the Gospel—thus preserving the Japhethic hierarchy.

The Reformation did challenge Catholic authority, but not its biblical ethnography. Japhethic/European/white notions were deeply intertwined with scriptural exegesis, history and providential interpretations. Even if reformers rejected papal authority, the idea that Europe was God's instrument of expansion fit Protestant ambitions and wasn't seen as "wrong." The social, political, and economic benefits of maintaining the ideology reinforced its persistence.

Some Protestants eventually questioned the morality of slavery or colonial conquest—but did not challenge the Japhethic framework. In other words, Protestant reform was about theology and church practice. It was not about undoing the Eurocentric interpretations of Genesis 9–10.

The Protestant Reformation did not correct the Japhethic hierarchy, because it was primarily concerned with theological and ecclesiastical reform, not ethnography or geopolitics. The Eurocentric, "Japheth-superior" worldview was compatible with Protestant expansion, so it persisted and even migrated into Protestant colonial ideology, reinforcing European dominance without the Vatican as mediator.

The <u>REAL Truth</u>: God's Kingdom Diversity, Equity and Inclusion *(DEI)* through Jesus:

While Europeans—Japhethites—are not biologically part of Jesus' genealogy through Abraham, that was never God's ultimate plan for salvation. God's covenant was never meant to entrench racial hierarchies or justify empire; it was always meant to **redeem all nations**. The promise to Abraham stands unbroken: *"In your seed all nations of the earth shall be blessed"* (Genesis 22:18). This is not a selective blessing for Europe, nor a divine warrant for conquest, colonization, or racial domination. It is the blueprint of God's kingdom—spiritual, inclusive, and subversive of human hierarchies.

The New Testament makes this abundantly clear. Jesus Christ came not to uphold Japhethic expansion or to dwell in the tents of Shem as a tool of empire, but to bring salvation to all peoples, across every lineage and every nation. Through Him, Shem's covenant becomes universal, and the supposed curse of Ham—any misreading thereof—is overturned. The gospel of Jesus tears down human-imposed hierarchies and exposes the lie that one nation or race is divinely destined to rule over another.

Even as European powers wrapped conquest, slavery, and colonization in the banner of Christianity, the kingdom of God remained antithetical to such tyranny. Christ's genealogy, culminating in Israel yet extending to all humanity through His life, death, and resurrection, reveals that covenantal blessing is **not inherited by skin, blood, or imperial might—but received by faith and obedience to God**. The tents of Shem were never meant to be occupied as a staging ground for domination; they were a symbol of covenant, mercy, and inclusion, now extended to every tribe and nation through Christ.

This is the prophetic truth: all human claims to racial or cultural supremacy are counterfeit before God. Japheth's enlargement, Ham's supposed curse, Shem's spiritual inheritance—all are subsumed under

66

the kingdom inaugurated by Jesus. Empire, conquest, and racial hierarchy are revealed as fallen distortions of God's promise. The gospel turns the tables: the last are made first, the marginalized are exalted, and all nations are called to dwell under the rule of the true King.

Acts 10:34–35 – God shows no favoritism; Gentiles (like Cornelius, a Roman) receive the Holy Spirit.

Ephesians 2:12–13 "You were at that time separated from Christ... strangers to the covenants of promise...But now in Christ Jesus you who once were far off have been brought near by the blood of Christ."

Galatians 3:28 "There is neither Jew nor Greek (Black, Brown or White)... for you are all one in Christ Jesus."

Thus, Japheth's descendants are fully included spiritually by faith in Jesus, just as Shem's and Ham's descendants are.

Why Satan Stirred Anger in Japheth: *Europeans and White People*

I truly believe that, from the very moment Noah pronounced the blessing in Genesis 9:27— *"May God enlarge Japheth, and let him dwell in the tents of Shem"*—the spiritual battlefield was set. God's intent was clear: Japheth's descendants were to grow, not in pride or force, but in covenantal alignment, humility, and faith. They were to dwell in Shem's tents, entering the blessing of Israel through obedience, not through domination. The promise was prophetic: all nations, through Christ, were to participate in God's covenantal plan, fulfilling Abraham's call that *"in your seed all nations of the earth shall be blessed"* (Genesis 22:18).

Satan, however, understood the weight of this blessing. He saw the potential for Japheth's expansion to be twisted, and he set to work corrupting God's order. Instead of entering the tents of Shem as a guest under God's authority, Japheth's descendants—Europeans—were tempted to seize them. They were encouraged to invert blessing into power, covenant into conquest, spiritual inheritance into imperial entitlement. This perversion took root in Rome, where the papacy fused spiritual authority with temporal dominion. The Vatican sanctified conquest, baptized empire, colonized, and later racial hierarchies as if they were providential. Jesuits, Franciscans, and other missionaries carried this deception to Asia, Africa, and the Americas, using conversion as the instrument of domination, while claiming to fulfill God's covenantal blessing.

The ethnographic framework of Genesis 10 provided Satan a scaffold for racialized ideology. Japheth was celebrated as culturally refined and expansionist; Shem retained spiritual primacy but was politically subordinated; Ham's descendants—especially Sub-Saharan Africans—were cast as cursed or servile, while Upper Africans were selectively valorized as assimilable. This allowed colonial powers to divide the world into spiritual and racial hierarchies, cloaking greed, slavery, and genocide in the guise of covenantal mission. The "dwelling in Shem's tents" motif became twisted: it was no longer a symbol of inclusion in God's covenant through Christ, but a justification for imperial entitlement and racialized domination.

Protestant nations inherited the same counterfeit vision. England, Holland, and later America carried forward Japhethic ideology without the papal framework, yet the logic remained identical: conquest and conversion intertwined, cultural erasure justified by a distorted theology, and racial hierarchies maintained under the guise of divine mandate. Sub-Saharan Africans were enslaved, Indigenous Americans displaced, and Asian societies pressured to assimilate European norms—all in the name of God, yet serving Satan's deception.

And yet, the prophetic truth stands unshaken. God's covenant cannot be corrupted. Japheth's enlargement was never intended to rule through domination, Ham's descendants were never cursed beyond redemption, and Shem's inheritance was never meant to be a tool of oppression. Jesus

Christ fulfills the promise to Abraham: through Him, all nations are blessed, not by the sword or the empire, but through faith and obedience. The tents of Shem belong to God; they are meant for blessing, not exploitation.

Satan's counterfeit is exposed in every hierarchy, every empire, every ideology that claims divine sanction for human domination. But the kingdom of God overturns this false order. The humble are exalted, the oppressed are vindicated, and all nations—Japheth, Ham, and Shem alike—are invited into covenantal fellowship through Christ. God's plan is not empire; it is redemption. It is not conquest; it is communion. The tents of Shem will be filled, not by force, but by faithful obedience.

And this is the prophetic call: every claim of racial or cultural supremacy, every perversion of covenant into conquest, every abuse of spiritual authority for human gain, will be overturned. Japheth's enlargement will be restored to its true purpose—not domination, but blessing. Ham's descendants, wrongly marginalized, will receive justice and honor. Shem's line will shine through Christ as intended, and all nations will dwell together under the reign of the true King. Satan may counterfeit, he may co-opt, he may attempt to rewrite the covenant—but he cannot thwart God's plan. The tents of Shem belong to the Lord, and they will be filled with every tribe, nation, and tongue that submits in faith to Christ.

The Error of Replacement: A Kingdom Vision Beyond Supersessionism

For me, replacement theology—often called *supersessionism*—is not just an abstract theological debate. It strikes at the very heart of how we understand the Kingdom of God. Supersessionism assumes that God has abandoned His covenant with Israel, transferring all of His promises exclusively to the Church. In this view, Israel's story is finished, its covenant exhausted, and its blessings now redirected elsewhere.

But the gospel of the Kingdom tells a different story. Jesus did not come to abolish Israel's covenant; He came to fulfill it. As He Himself declared: *"Do not think that I have come to abolish the Law or the Prophets; I have not come to abolish them but to fulfill them"* (Matthew 5:17). Christ is not the end of Israel's calling but its embodiment and fulfillment. As Paul reminds us, "For all the promises of God find their Yes in him" (2 Corinthians 1:20).

The Kingdom of God is not built on exclusion but on expansion. In Christ, Jew and Gentile are reconciled, the dividing wall of hostility torn down, and one new humanity created (Ephesians 2:14–16). Paul dares to call this people "the Israel of God" (Galatians 6:16). This is not a *replacement Israel* but a renewed Israel—an Israel now widened to embrace all nations. The root remains Israel, while Gentiles are graciously grafted in by faith (Romans 11:17–18).

This is why supersessionism is such a distortion. It imagines God as discarding one people in order to choose another, when in fact the Kingdom reveals a God whose faithfulness endures and whose covenant never fails.

Scholars today have begun to reckon with this distortion. R. Kendall Soulen describes supersessionism as "a profound misrepresentation of the God of Israel," noting that it pushes Israel to the margins when Israel is in fact central to the drama of salvation (*The God of Israel and Christian Theology*, 2008, p. 31). N. T. Wright emphasizes that God's covenant with Abraham was always aimed at blessing *all nations*, and that Jesus is the one who brings this covenant to completion, not cancellation (*Paul and the Faithfulness of God*, 2013, p. 832). Miroslav Volf, writing pastorally out of his own experience of ethnic division, insists that God's Kingdom cannot be built on exclusionary logic but must be an embrace that gathers Jew and Gentile alike into one family (*Exclusion and Embrace*, 1996, p. 52).

Taken together, these insights affirm what the Spirit has opened to me: the Church is not Israel's replacement but Israel's expansion. The promises to Abraham remain alive; the root is not cut off. In Christ, the nations are grafted in—not as usurpers, but as welcomed participants in God's eternal covenant.

The error of supersessionism matters because it mirrors the same spirit of division that has plagued the world through race, class, and cultural superiority. Just as racism falsely elevates one group over another, supersessionism falsely elevates the Church over Israel. But the Kingdom vision proclaims something radically different: that all are gathered into one body, one covenant family, under one Messiah.

The Kingdom's Response to Division, Supremacy, and Resentment

There is a reason why recent events—most notably the tragic assassination of Charlie Kirk—cut so deeply, why the rhetoric he championed and the surge of Christian Nationalism set off alarm bells in my spirit. What we are witnessing is not merely political turbulence or partisan noise; it is a spiritual phenomenon, the visible eruption of division, pride, and manipulation that has plagued humanity since Eden. These are not isolated incidents; they are the fruit of a persistent, age-old strategy—a strategy designed to corrupt, to seduce, and to fracture the unity that God intended for His people.

And in our time, this strategy has found a new and dangerous vector: the exploitation of youth, particularly Generation Z. The young are being weaponized spiritually, culturally, and ideologically. They are fed narratives that blend pride with entitlement, fear with anger, and superficial righteousness with cultural aggression. Their idealism, their hunger for justice, and their yearning for identity are being hijacked, turned into instruments of division rather than instruments of God's kingdom.

From the very foundation of human history, God established an order in Genesis 9–10: Japheth was to be enlarged, Shem entrusted with the covenant, and Ham positioned within the blessing of God's promise. This was never meant to create domination, hierarchy, or division; it was a framework for covenantal obedience, blessing, and the extension of God's kingdom to all nations. Yet, as history shows—from the papacy and the rise of Europe to the Protestant colonial empires and the trans-Atlantic slave trade—Satan has sought to invert this divine order at every turn. He thrives on pride, ambition, and the corruption of blessing into power.

Just as Japheth's enlargement was distorted into conquest, Shem's inheritance into subordination, and Ham's descendants into marginalization, the next generation is being co-opted into ideological, spiritual, and cultural frameworks that twist their gifts into instruments of division rather than blessing. The manipulation of youth today mirrors the spiritual logic of empire: pride masquerades as righteousness, allegiance to ideology as covenantal fidelity, and rebellion as moral authority.

This exploitation manifests in three interlocking ways:

First, identity hijacking. Generation Z is being taught to define themselves not through Christ or covenantal truth, but through political, cultural, and social allegiances. Their idealism—God-given, vibrant, and prophetic—is weaponized, turning them into enforcers of ideologies rather than ambassadors of the kingdom. Just as Japhethites were tempted to claim Shem's tents through force, young people are tempted to claim influence, status, and moral authority through prideful allegiance rather than obedience to God.

Second, spiritualized pride and false superiority. Youth are seduced into believing that righteousness is measured by dominance, exclusion, or control. This mirrors the historical distortion of Genesis 9–10, where Europe claimed Japhethic supremacy, subjugated Ham's descendants, and subordinated Shem's spiritual inheritance. Today, social media, pop culture, and ideological movements amplify pride and division, shaping young hearts into carriers of conflict rather than vessels of blessing.

Third, fear, anger, and division as control mechanisms.

Generation Z is being conditioned to respond to the world through hostility, anxiety, and reactionary posture, rather than through discernment, humility, and kingdom-minded engagement. Satan has always sought to fracture communities and turn youth against one another. Just as conquest and colonialism were justified by distorted theology, the spiritual and cultural manipulation of youth today disguises division as moral duty, anger as justice, and rebellion as righteous zeal.

This explains why contemporary flashpoints—such as the assassination of Charlie Kirk, the rise of Christian Nationalism, and other political spectacles—are more than news stories. They are spiritual barometers, revealing the deep currents of pride, manipulation, and counterfeit covenant in the present age. The tents of Shem, meant to be sacred spaces of blessing and covenant, are being misappropriated as platforms for domination and ideological conquest.

Yet the prophetic and kingdom truth remains unshaken: God's order is covenantal, not coercive. Japheth's enlargement is fulfilled in obedience, not in domination; Shem's inheritance is spiritual, not subordinated by ideology; Ham's descendants are blessed, not marginalized. Generation Z is not a tool for empire or ideological warfare—they are vessels for revival, bearers of blessing, and instruments for covenantal justice.

The call is clear: the Church must rise in discernment, teaching youth to dwell rightly in Shem's tents—not as conquerors, manipulators, or enforcers, but as covenantal participants in God's kingdom. They must learn to channel their energy, idealism, and influence through obedience, humility, and the gospel, so that the next generation will be a force for reconciliation, restoration, and blessing across all nations.

This is the prophetic mandate: Satan may counterfeit covenant to pride, division, and domination, but the true King—Jesus Christ—will restore God's order. Japheth will enlarge through blessing, not force; Shem will shine through covenantal faithfulness; Ham will be vindicated and honored. Generation Z, when trained in the ways of the kingdom, will turn what was exploited into instruments of redemption, making the tents of Shem a dwelling place of blessing for all nations.

Racial Supremacy Movements

These ideologies—that Europeans or white people are God's uniquely chosen by birthright, ancestry, or skin color—are not merely wrong; they are a spiritual abomination. They seize the language of covenant, blessing, and divine promise and twist it into a weapon of pride, domination, and oppression. This is the same strategy Satan has employed since Genesis: taking God's covenantal words and perverting them to empower human ambition and justify injustice. Historically, it fueled the Hamitic Hypothesis, the Transatlantic Slave Trade, segregation, and colonial domination (Goldenberg 171; Sanders 98). Europe claimed Japhethic enlargement not in humility, but in conquest; Shem's tents were reinterpreted as European territory; Ham's descendants were devalued and exploited. Scripture itself was co-opted to serve the empire rather than God's kingdom.

Today, the same spiritual logic is being weaponized against youth, particularly Generation Z. Their energy, idealism, and thirst for justice are being manipulated through social media, political rhetoric, and cultural ideology. They are told that power, influence, and identity come through allegiance to tribe, nation, or ideology rather than through covenant with Christ. Pride is dressed as righteousness, anger as moral clarity, and division as virtue. The tents of Shem, meant to be spaces of blessing and spiritual inheritance, are being occupied through manipulation rather than faith. Generation Z is being trained to assert dominance over others in the name of ideology—mirroring centuries of

Japhethic distortion, yet under the guise of morality, activism, or patriotism.

Theological truth, however, stands unshaken. In Christ, **all nations are blessed, all peoples are included, and every tribe and tongue is invited into the Kingdom** (Revelation 5:9). Covenant is never inherited by skin, power, or human hierarchy—it is accessed through faith, obedience, and covenantal alignment with God. Japheth's enlargement, Shem's inheritance, and Ham's blessing are not privileges to be seized; they are instruments of blessing to be stewarded. Satan seeks to invert this order, turning blessing into arrogance, obedience into entitlement, and covenant into conquest.

The prophetic call is urgent: the Church must rise as a fortress of truth, guiding youth into covenantal wisdom, exposing the lies of racial, cultural, and ideological supremacy, and reclaiming the tents of Shem for God's Kingdom. Generation Z must be taught that their identity is found in Christ, not in empire, ideology, or manipulation. They must learn to wield influence through blessing rather than coercion, through faith rather than pride, through covenant rather than conquest.

This is the spiritual battleground of our age. The historical distortions that justified slavery, colonialism, and racial hierarchy are now being replayed in the hearts and minds of young people. But the Kingdom of God overturns every counterfeit: the last are made first, the marginalized are exalted, and all nations are called to dwell under God's righteous rule. Japheth's enlargement must be redeemed to serve blessing, Shem's inheritance must shine through covenant, and Ham's descendants must be restored to honor. The tents of Shem belong to God alone, and the Church must rise to defend them, teaching all generations to dwell rightly, humbly, and faithfully in the fullness of His Kingdom.

Colonial Christianity

Rather than fostering mutual submission under Christ, colonial and nationalistic forms of Christianity have too often imposed cultural conformity as if obedience to Christ were synonymous with obedience to empire. This distortion conflates gospel truth with human power, turning faith into a tool for domination rather than an instrument of grace. The cross, meant to dismantle hierarchy and pride, is co-opted to justify conquest, cultural erasure, and the subjugation of those deemed "other." European expansion, Protestant missions, and nationalist movements alike have all too often weaponized Scripture to sanctify assimilation, converting obedience into a mandate for cultural homogeneity rather than covenantal faithfulness.

Miroslav Volf reminds us that God's Kingdom is not constructed on coercion or domination but on embrace and reconciliation: *"To be embraced is to be included in the community that mirrors God's own self-giving love, and exclusion is the antithesis of this divine vision"* (Volf 55). The gospel of Jesus Christ calls for covenantal inclusion, not imperial imposition. Christ does not homogenize; He unifies. He binds together diverse peoples, languages, and cultures into a single body, where distinctiveness is not erased but honored, and where every tribe and nation can dwell in covenantal blessing.

Colonial Christianity—whether Catholic or Protestant—twisted the tents of Shem into instruments of power, turning Japhethic expansion into empire, Ham's descendants into laborers or subjects, and Shem's inheritance into a stage for European dominance. Faith was no longer a path to reconciliation but a justification for hierarchy. This inversion of the gospel is precisely what Satan seeks: to replace covenantal unity with coercion, blessing with subjugation, and grace with pride.

The prophetic call is clear: God's Kingdom cannot be reduced to cultural or ethnic conformity. Christ's mission is to gather all nations, all peoples, and all generations under His covenant—not to erase their particularities, but to align their lives with His Kingdom purposes. True enlargement, Japhethic or otherwise, is exercised in humility, not in cultural imposition. The tents of Shem are meant for blessing, not occupation; for inclusion, not domination. Every act of forced assimilation, every claim that faith requires cultural surrender, is a counterfeit of Christ's mission.

To live prophetically today is to resist this false gospel of cultural supremacy. It is to proclaim that the Kingdom of God honors diversity within covenantal unity, that Japheth, Ham, and Shem alike are called into blessing, and that the tents of Shem are spaces of reconciliation, not instruments of conquest. The gospel calls for justice, mercy, and humility; it calls for embrace, not coercion. And in this, the true Church mirrors the self-giving love of God Himself, where every nation, tribe, and tongue can dwell together under Christ's reign.

Modern Resentment and Hostility

Anger over perceived exclusion, whether real or imagined, can foster hostility toward those perceived as "other," or even toward God Himself. This resentment is often exploited by powers of pride and fear, turning the natural longing for recognition into a weapon of division. Martin Luther King Jr. identified this as the core danger of human sin in society: a failure to see the inherent dignity of all, allowing pride and jealousy to dominate the human heart (King 78).

Taken together, these forces—racial supremacy, cultural coercion, and resentment—operate like spiritual currents that oppose God's redemptive plan. They are modern iterations of the same demonic strategy we first encounter in Genesis 3 and 4, where Satan exploits pride and disobedience to fracture human unity. Just as Cain's jealousy led to violence, and Babel's pride led to dispersion, today's ideologies threaten both the Church and the broader human family with division.

Yet the Kingdom of God provides a radically different vision. In Christ, no ethnic group is inherently superior, no culture is preferred, and no history of exclusion is final. Paul's teaching in Galatians 3:28 dismantles human hierarchies: *"There is neither Jew nor Greek, slave nor free, male nor female, for you are all one in Christ Jesus."* This unity is not theoretical—it is covenantal, rooted in the blood of Christ, and prophetic in scope. Gentiles, formerly outside God's covenant, are now welcomed; descendants of Ham, often marginalized and misrepresented, are included through faith (Rahab); the root of Israel remains central, with all nations grafted into the tree of promise (Romans 11:17–24).

Christian Nationalism and racialized ideologies, in contrast, invert this Kingdom vision. They mistake privilege for blessing and hierarchy for holiness. From a pastoral perspective, this is profoundly tragic because it obscures the gospel's invitation to repentance, reconciliation, and radical love. The Kingdom calls every believer—Jew and Gentile, Black, Brown, and White—to resist these forces, to live as agents of God's inclusive justice, and to bear witness to the truth that all peoples are heirs of the covenant through Christ.

Ultimately, the challenge before the Church is both spiritual and practical: to confront these ideologies not with human rhetoric alone but with Kingdom truth, lived out in daily acts of inclusion, reconciliation, and worship. The stakes are high because this is not merely about social harmony—it is about manifesting the very heart of God, who desires a people united across tribe, tongue, and nation under the reign of Christ. As Martin Luther King Jr. so often reminded us, God's vision is for a beloved community where justice, love, and equality reign. When we succumb to the allure of racial supremacy, cultural domination, or resentful pride, we are participating in the very schemes of division that the gospel calls us to dismantle. The Kingdom of God is where inclusion, reconciliation, and mutual honor are the marks of true discipleship.

Application for Today

The anger, confusion, and strife we witness in the world today—racial tension, nationalism, anti-Semitism, and ideological polarization—are not merely political or cultural problems; they are spiritual battles waged in the invisible realm. Satan seeks to divide, manipulate, and corrupt, preying on pride, resentment, and fear. Generation Z, with their idealism, moral hunger, and thirst for justice, has become a prime target. Young hearts are being exploited, their energy co-opted to carry forward the very divisions God intended to heal.

White people—Japheth, Europeans, and their descendants—must confront a profound truth: inclusion in God's covenant and salvation is by **grace alone**, not by genealogy, race, or power. Satan whispers lies of entitlement and superiority, stirring anger and resentment when pride feels threatened or when cultural influence seems diminished. God never excluded Japheth; the Messiah came to bring every nation into covenantal blessing. The call for Japheth is not conquest, dominance, or cultural coercion—but humility: to dwell in Shem's tents through Christ, receiving blessing spiritually, not attempting to seize it by human strength.

The genealogy of Jesus Christ tells this story of redemption and inclusion. Shem provides the Messiah, the vessel of covenantal promise; Ham is redeemed, exemplified through figures like Rahab, brought into God's plan despite human marginalization; and Japheth joins spiritually through the expansion of the Gospel, called to live not as conqueror, but as steward of blessing. This is the Kingdom vision: God's covenant moves outward, uniting all nations through obedience, faith, and reconciliation.

For people of color, as for all God's children, Satan's strategy is the same: to divide and conquer. He seeks to keep anger simmering, pride festering, unforgiveness holding hearts captive, and resentment fueling cycles of racial tension. He whispers lies: some lives are worth more than others, some voices deserve to be heard while others are silenced. He weaponizes history, ideology, and social movements to foment discord, feeding off wounded hearts and disoriented youth. Generation Z, connected across digital networks, is particularly vulnerable to these manipulations, often carrying the spiritual weight of inherited anger, cultural expectation, and the counterfeit promises of power.

But Jesus Christ shatters every chain the enemy forges. Where Satan plants division, Jesus plants reconciliation. Where he fans the flames of resentment, Jesus pours the living water of forgiveness. Where human pride insists on superiority, Christ insists on humility. In the gospel, race, history, and human sin do not define worth; every heart submitted to Christ is incorporated into a family that transcends the world's divisions. Every young person, every Generation Z believer, is called into covenantal identity, empowered to resist the lies of superiority, victimhood, or resentment, and to live as agents of Kingdom reconciliation.

In Christ, no bitterness can stand, no pride can dominate, and no injustice can hold ultimate sway. Japheth is redeemed not through conquest but through covenantal blessing. Ham is restored not through manipulation but through faithfulness. Shem's covenant is not appropriated for empire but extended to all nations. Christ unites humanity under His rule, defeating Satan's schemes not with force, but with the transforming power of grace, mercy, and Kingdom love.

This is the prophetic mandate for our time: the Church must rise to teach Generation Z that their true identity is in Christ, not in ideology, race, or cultural allegiance. They must learn to dwell in the tents of Shem rightly: with humility, obedience, and a heart for blessing all nations. They are called to be witnesses of God's Kingdom in a fractured world, agents of reconciliation where Satan sows division, and carriers of covenantal truth where pride and resentment seek to reign. The gospel is the antidote to every lie of superiority, every spark of racial or nationalistic pride, and every tool of manipulation. In Christ, all divisions fall, all nations are included, and the Kingdom of God is revealed in power, justice, and mercy.

Race is a Human Construction and Why This Issue is Spiritual

The Bible never defines humanity in terms of "race" as we understand the concept today. Scripture speaks in the language of **families, tribes, tongues, and nations**—categories rooted in covenant, community, and God's ordering of creation (see Genesis 10; Revelation 7:9). Humanity is understood relationally and spiritually, not hierarchically by skin color or ancestry. Modern racial categories are human inventions, forged in the context of European expansion, colonialism, and empire, and have historically been wielded to **justify hierarchy, exploitation, and domination** (see *The Forging of Races: Race and Scripture in the Protestant Atlantic World, 1600–2000*, Cambridge University Press & Assessment).

Paul warns in Ephesians 6:12 that **"we do not wrestle against flesh and blood, but against the rulers, against the authorities, against the cosmic powers over this present darkness..."** This reveals that evil operates not merely through individuals but through **systems, structures, and ideologies**—social, political, and spiritual. The modern invention of race has been co-opted into one of these fallen systems, weaponized to divide, oppress, and deceive humanity, turning God's good creation into a tool of pride and control.

In this sense, race is not simply an idea; it is a spiritual and social structure opposed to God's Kingdom. It is a counterfeit order, a shadow system that seeks to invert God's covenantal design. Christian theologians and historians—such as those writing in *Race and Scripture*—have demonstrated how Scripture has been **misread and mobilized** historically to support racial ideologies, even though the biblical text itself never teaches these categories. The misuse of Genesis 9–10, the Hamitic Hypothesis, and colonial interpretations of Noah's curse are prime examples of how Scripture has been distorted to sanctify human oppression.

The prophetic truth is clear: God's Kingdom is **not built on race, hierarchy, or coercion**. It is founded on covenant, faith, and inclusion in Christ. Japheth is to dwell in Shem's tents through humility and obedience, Ham is to be restored and honored, and Shem's inheritance is to shine as a blessing to all nations. Any human attempt to define value, access, or authority by skin, lineage, or power is a counterfeit of God's order—a tool of Satan to divide, mislead, and enslave hearts.

The Church must rise prophetically to **expose these false systems**, teach the biblical reality of covenantal belonging, and reclaim God's vision for humanity. Every person, every tribe, and every nation finds true identity not in color, culture, or empire, but in Christ. The Kingdom overturns every human hierarchy, dismantles every structure of oppression, and unites all creation in covenantal blessing, justice, and mercy.

The Enemy's Exploitation of Japheth's Destiny in History

From Eden onward, the serpent has always twisted God's words to entice humanity to grasp at power: *"Did God really say…? For God knows that when you eat of it you will be like God"* (Genesis 3:1–5). Satan takes God's blessings and redirects them into corrupted systems. What God meant for enlargement (Genesis 9:27), Satan perverts into conquest. What God meant for covenant blessing through Shem, Satan distorts into resentment and anti-Semitism. What God meant for Ham's redemption, Satan turns into cycles of slavery and oppression.

Shem: *Attacked Through Anti-Semitism and Replacement Theology*

The Crusades (11th–13th centuries): While presented as holy wars to reclaim the Holy Land, many Crusaders massacred Jewish communities in Europe on their way to Jerusalem. This was fueled by the lie that Shem's covenant role was obsolete and that Japheth's sword could replace God's blessing with empire (Zechariah 2:8).

The Spanish Inquisition (15th century): Jews were forced to convert or be expelled from Spain. Here, Satan whispered again: erase Shem's distinct witness, sever Israel from covenantal identity.

The Holocaust (20th century): Six million Jews were murdered in an industrialized genocide. Hitler's ideology was openly anti-Semitic, but beneath it was the same ancient hatred: an attempt to annihilate Shem's covenant line (Romans 11:28–29).

Anti-Semitism is not just prejudice—*it is a spiritual war against God's promises to Shem. Satan knows that God's covenant faithfulness to Israel is unbreakable, so he unleashes violence to make it appear fragile.*

Ham: *Enslaved and Marginalized to Prolong the "Curse"*

The Transatlantic Slave Trade (16th–19th centuries): European powers kidnapped and enslaved millions of Africans, justifying it with a twisted reading of Noah's curse (Genesis 9:25). Though the curse applied only to Canaan, Satan weaponized the misinterpretation to enslave Ham's descendants, seeking to chain them permanently under bondage.

Colonialism in Africa and the Americas: Entire nations were subjected to foreign control, their cultures suppressed, their people exploited. This systemic oppression flowed from a demonic lie: Ham cannot be redeemed, only ruled. Yet Scripture declares: *"Christ redeemed us from the curse by becoming a curse for us"* (Galatians 3:13).

Jim Crow and Apartheid (19th–20th centuries): Even after abolition, structures of segregation and discrimination persisted, echoing Satan's attempt to keep Ham marginalized and excluded from fullness in Christ (Acts 8:27–39 as testimony of Ham's inclusion).

Ham's story *is not one of perpetual curse but of redemption. The enemy fears this, so he perpetuates slavery and racism to mute Ham's prophetic song.*

Japheth: *Tempted Into Conquest and Domination*

Roman Empire (4th–5th centuries): When Christianity was embraced by Constantine, Japheth's enlargement merged with imperial expansion. Instead of dwelling humbly in Shem's tents, Japheth often tried to occupy them.

European Colonial Expansion (15th–19th centuries): Nations like Spain, Portugal, England, and the Netherlands claimed divine right to seize lands across Africa, Asia, and the Americas. Satan's lie here: enlargement equals domination. But Genesis 9:27 calls Japheth to enlargement in *dwelling with Shem*, not dispossessing him.

Modern Nationalisms (19th–20th centuries): Japheth's enlargement turned inward, creating ideologies of racial superiority (Nazism, white supremacy). These are not neutral ideologies; they are demonic distortions of Japheth's prophetic destiny.

Japheth was meant to be enlarged *for blessing, exploration, and partnership. Instead, Satan tempts Japheth into Babel-like empire building (Genesis 11:4), grasping power apart from God.*

Prophetic Reversal in Christ

For Shem: *"Has God rejected his people? By no means!"* (Romans 11:1). Anti-Semitism is a direct contradiction of God's irrevocable covenant.

For Ham: The blood of Jesus breaks every curse and silences every chain (Galatians 3:13–14). Ham is redeemed, not doomed.

For Japheth: True enlargement comes only when Japheth dwells in Shem's tents—in covenantal humility, grafted into Israel's promises through Messiah (Romans 11:17–24).

The vision of Revelation 7:9 shows the divine endgame: Shem, Ham, and Japheth reconciled before the throne, clothed in white, waving palm branches, proclaiming together, "Salvation belongs to our God and to the Lamb!" Satan's distortions will be silenced, and God's design for the nations will be fulfilled.

History bears witness that anti-Semitism, slavery, colonialism, racism and empire are not mere human accidents—*they are satanic distortions of God's prophecy concerning Shem, Ham, and Japheth.* Satan whispers jealousy into Japheth's heart against Shem, chains Ham under a false curse, and tempts Japheth into empire. But Christ has broken these lies. In Him, Japheth's enlargement, Shem's blessing, and Ham's redemption converge into one redeemed family at the throne of God.

The Solution is the Kingdom of God

A Kingdom Identity

From the dawn of human history, God established covenantal order in Genesis 9–10: Japheth was to be enlarged, Shem entrusted with covenant, and Ham positioned within blessing. This was never intended to justify hierarchy, domination, or oppression. Japheth's enlargement was to be exercised in humility, Shem's inheritance was to shine spiritually, and Ham's descendants were to be honored and restored. Yet Satan has continually sought to invert God's design. Where God intended blessing, unity, and covenantal order, Satan sowed pride, jealousy, and division.

Historically, this distortion took shape in empire, colonialism, and racial ideology. Europeans—claiming Japhethic enlargement—subjugated Ham's descendants, manipulated Shem's covenant, and reinterpreted Scripture to sanctify conquest. The Hamitic Hypothesis, the misuse of Noah's curse, the Transatlantic Slave Trade, and colonial domination are vivid examples of Scripture twisted to justify human pride, hierarchy, and oppression. The tents of Shem, meant to be spaces of blessing, became theaters of cultural conquest; Japheth's enlargement was wielded as empire, not obedience; Ham's descendants were devalued and exploited.

Satan's strategy is not merely historical; it is spiritual and ongoing. Today, Generation Z stands at the frontline of these same spiritual battles. Their energy, idealism, and moral convictions are targeted by lies, division, and pride. Social media, ideology, and political rhetoric are leveraged to twist their zeal into instruments of factionalism, racial resentment, and cultural coercion. Satan seeks to replicate centuries of human distortion—Japheth's pride, Shem's subversion, Ham's marginalization—within the hearts and minds of this generation.

Yet the Kingdom of God calls forth a radical correction. Scripture proclaims: **Ephesians 2:14–16**—"For He Himself is our peace, who has made the two groups one and has destroyed the barrier, the dividing wall of hostility…" and **Galatians 3:28**—"There is neither Jew nor Greek, slave nor free, male nor female, for you are all one in Christ Jesus." Through Christ, Japheth's jealousy and pride are healed; blessing is received in humility, not force. Shem's covenant is honored in obedience, not domination. Ham's redemption is affirmed as complete, equal, and covenantally secured.

Generation Z, uniquely gifted for connectivity, justice, and moral clarity, is called to embrace this Kingdom vision. They must reject the counterfeit ideologies of racial, nationalistic, and cultural supremacy that have long distorted God's covenantal order. Their convictions about justice, equality, and inclusion are not merely political preferences; they are instruments of Kingdom restoration when aligned with humility, covenantal obedience, and the gospel of Christ.

The Kingdom does more than reconcile individuals; it dismantles systems of oppression. It dethrones pride, empire, and human hierarchy while uniting all peoples in covenantal blessing. Japheth, Ham, and Shem alike are called into their God-given roles: Japheth humbly enlarged to bless, Shem faithfully stewarding covenant, Ham fully restored and honored. In Christ, barriers fall, hostility is destroyed, and all generations—including the youth of Generation Z—become agents of reconciliation, justice, and covenantal peace.

This is the prophetic mandate: the Church must expose Satan's counterfeit systems, reclaim the tents of Shem, and teach every generation that identity, authority, and blessing are found only in Christ. Japheth's enlargement is redeemed through obedience, not conquest. Shem's inheritance shines in faithfulness, not coercion. Ham's descendants are restored, vindicated, and fully included. Every human-made division—race, culture, history, or ideology—is dismantled, and God's Kingdom is revealed in power, mercy, and covenantal unity.

The gospel overturns the lies of empire and the distortions of pride. The Kingdom unites, restores, and reconciles. Generation Z is not merely an audience to this vision—they are called to embody it. They are to dwell rightly in the tents of Shem, carry the blessing of Japheth in humility, honor the redemption of Ham, and advance God's covenantal justice across a fractured world. In this, the Kingdom of God triumphs—not through human force, but through Christ's grace, mercy, and transformative power.

The Hope for Japheth's Descendants

Even though Japheth's line has historically been misled, there is profound hope and redemption. The prophecy of Genesis 9:27 is fulfilled not through conquest or human ambition, but through the Gospel: Japheth dwells in the tents of Shem by entering covenant with Jesus, the greater Son of Shem. This is not a partial inclusion; it is full participation in God's covenantal blessing. Europeans and other Gentiles are called to repent—not merely of overt sins, but of pride, retaliation, and entitlement—and to embrace their true place: not as conquerors, but as **co-heirs with Shem and Ham through Christ** (Romans 11:17–24).

Yes, race as a system was largely constructed through Japheth's historical expansion, used to divide, exploit, and oppress. Yet through Jesus, the dividing wall is broken. The power of human jealousy, retaliation, and domination is undone. In the Kingdom, Shem, Ham, and Japheth are reconciled into **one new humanity**, where every former distinction used to justify inequality is redeemed and transformed.

This reconciliation is not theoretical—it is covenantal, spiritual, and lived. Japheth learns humility and receives blessing in alignment with God's will; Shem's covenant calling is honored without pride or superiority; Ham's descendants are fully restored and affirmed. In Christ, no line is marginalized, no voice is silenced, and no history of division can stand against God's reconciling love.

The prophetic and pastoral call is clear: we must live as a redeemed people, proclaiming that all humanity—regardless of ancestry, tribe, or history—is united in Christ. We must confront the lies that once justified division, dismantle systems of pride and racial hierarchy, and embrace the covenantal reality of **one humanity in the Kingdom of God**. This is the fulfillment of God's promise: Japheth enlarged, Shem blessed, Ham restored—and all reconciled through the mercy and power of Jesus Christ.

Bigotry vs. Prejudice

Prejudice is literally a pre-judgment: the formation of an opinion about a person or people before any real knowledge of them, usually built on stereotype and assumption. The English word itself comes from the Latin *prae* ("before") and *judicium* ("judgment"), and the phenomenon is as old as sin. Scripture repeatedly shows how fallen human hearts create and harden divisions — from Cain and Abel to Ishmael and Isaac, Jacob and Esau — divisions that become the soil in which prejudice takes root. When that root deepens and hardens, it becomes bigotry: an obstinate, intolerant devotion to one's own group, opinions, or identity that expresses itself in hatred or systematic exclusion. Bigotry is prejudice weaponized; it is prejudice that has become a structure — encoded in laws, philosophies, and institutions — designed to preserve advantage and enforce inequality. In short, modern bigotry is not merely an attitude of the heart but a designed social architecture meant to maintain dominance.

It is essential to recognize that the modern map of racial categories — "white," "Black," "Asian," and the like — did not exist in biblical times. Biblical texts describe people by family, tribe, language, and nation; they do not articulate the modern biological or color-coded categories used to sort and rank human beings today. The modern racial system is a later construction largely shaped during the early modern and modern periods in Europe and the Atlantic world. Scholarship demonstrates that European thinkers, colonial administrators, and slave societies in the 17th–19th centuries formulated and propagated the categories and hierarchies that made slavery, dispossession, and racial domination intelligible and defensible. Works such as Winthrop Jordan's *White Over Black* and Nell Irvin Painter's *The History of White People* trace how "whiteness" was fashioned as a legal, social, and ideological category in tandem with colonial conquest and the transatlantic slave trade; Theodore W. Allen and others show how the "invention of the white race" functioned as a deliberate instrument of social control.[1][2][3]

This invention was not merely theoretical. It was authorized and enforced by legal and ecclesial instruments that European powers used to claim and divide the world. Papal bulls of the fifteenth century — for example, *Dum Diversas* (1452) and *Romanus Pontifex* (1455) — granted Iberian monarchs license to subdue "Saracens and pagans" and to take control of lands and peoples overseas; *Inter Caetera* (1493) allocated vast swaths of the Americas to Spain and Portugal and provided the juridical scaffolding for European claims of discovery and dispossession.[4][5][6] These documents did not by themselves create racial categories, but they helped legitimate a civilizational hierarchy that European states then translated into law and custom.

By the seventeenth century the legal vocabulary begins to reflect and enforce racial distinction. Colonial statutes — notably Virginia's slave and servant laws (e.g., the statute of 1705) — codified the status of Africans and indigenous peoples as "other," and helped to institutionalize lifelong servitude and racial caste in law and practice.[7][8] By the eighteenth and nineteenth centuries, a suite of so-called "scientific" theories — from polygenist accounts to phrenology and other racial sciences — claimed to find natural and biological bases for hierarchy, lending a pseudo-scientific patina to what had been a political and economic project from the start; critics such as Stephen Jay Gould have shown how those scientific claims were deeply biased and socially conditioned.[9][10]

Put plainly: the architecture of modern bigotry was engineered. It combined theological exegesis (sometimes abusive readings of Scripture), legal instruments, imperial practice, and pseudo-scientific justification to produce a durable system of racial domination. Contemporary theological and historical scholarship shows that Christianity was often complicit — sometimes actively, sometimes passively — in these constructions: church actors, missionaries, and ecclesial institutions frequently participated in or failed to resist the creation of racial hierarchies that contradicted the Bible's vision of humanity made in God's image and reconciled in Christ. Scholars such as Willie James Jennings and J. Kameron Carter trace how Christian imagination and theological categories were entangled with colonial projects and racial thought, while theologians like Esau McCaulley and Miroslav Volf offer theological resources for resisting and repairing those civic and ecclesial failures.[11][12][13][14]

Prophetically stated: what began as sin's ancient impulse to exclude and dominate was given new tools and new names in the early modern world. Prejudice — an ancient evil — was systematized into modern bigotry: designed, legally enforced, and theologically rationalized. Recognizing this is the first step toward dismantling it; Scripture calls the people of

God to a different work — the undoing of division, the breaking of curses, and the cultivation of a multi-ethnic, multi-tribal fellowship gathered before the Lamb (Revelation 7:9). Where history shows systems that dehumanize, the gospel summons practices and policies that restore human dignity and that reconfigure social life around the reconciling lordship of Christ.

The Spirit of Jealousy is Behind the Construction of Race

The underlying spirit behind the construction of modern racial categories is jealousy—a spiritual distortion aimed especially at Shem. Through Shem's line came Israel, and through Israel came the Messiah, Jesus Christ, the world's Redeemer (Genesis 12:1–3; Romans 9:4–5). Salvation and covenant blessings are channeled through Shem. Japheth, though prophetically promised enlargement (Genesis 9:27), was never meant to bypass Shem but to dwell in Shem's tents. Yet Satan, the deceiver from the beginning, stirred Japheth's descendants with a spirit of rivalry. It is the same spirit that moved Cain against Abel (Genesis 4:5–8), Esau against Jacob (Genesis 27:41), and Joseph's brothers against him (Genesis 37:4). The satanic whisper is always: *"If you cannot have the blessing, destroy the one who does."*

This jealousy not only targeted Shem through anti-Jewish violence, replacement theology, and attempts to erase Israel's covenant identity, but also targeted Ham. Though Ham's descendants were not cursed forever—the curse fell specifically on Canaan (Genesis 9:25)—the enemy sought to keep Ham under perpetual condemnation. For centuries, this lie was codified into law, theology, and custom: Ham's redemption was suppressed through slavery, segregation, and systemic oppression.

Ecclesial Complicity: *The Church's Mis-Cue*

What appalls me is that both the Catholic and Reformed churches, instead of discerning and resisting this satanic distortion, often legitimated it. The early church had already been given its cue in Pentecost (Acts 2:5–11), where people of every nation, tribe, and tongue heard the gospel in their own language. The apostles proclaimed a gospel that undid ethnic divisions: *"Here there is not Greek or Jew, circumcised or uncircumcised, barbarian, Scythian, slave or free, but Christ is all and in all"* (Colossians 3:11). Yet as the church became aligned with empire, it often failed to embody this radical inclusion.

The Catholic Church, through papal bulls like *Dum Diversas* (1452), *Romanus Pontifex* (1455), and *Inter Caetera* (1493), authorized Europeans to conquer, enslave, and dispossess non-Christian peoples. This became the so-called *Doctrine of Discovery*. Here, the church missed its prophetic vocation to defend the oppressed (Isaiah 1:17; Micah 6:8). Instead, it lent sacred authority to structures of domination.

The Reformed churches, though birthed in protest against Rome, often failed to correct this error. Martin Luther's Reformation rediscovered justification by faith but did not dismantle racialized hierarchies. In fact, some Reformers perpetuated anti-Jewish polemics, such as Luther's virulent treatise *On the Jews and Their Lies* (1543), which fueled later anti-Semitic violence. Calvin's Geneva, while advancing Scripture's authority, did not challenge the racialized economic order emerging through colonial expansion. Later Reformed traditions, particularly in the Netherlands, Britain, and North America, often supplied theological justification for slavery and segregation rather than resisting them.

As Willie James Jennings laments, the "Christian imagination" of the West became colonized; instead of a gospel of reconciliation, Christianity was harnessed to the architecture of race and empire (Jennings 2010, 6–10).

The Spiritual Dynamics

From a theological perspective, what emerged was not merely a social accident but the outworking of spiritual warfare:

Against Shem: Anti-Semitism, supersessionism, and ultimately the Holocaust sought to sever the covenant line. Yet Paul insists God's covenant with Israel is irrevocable (Romans 11:28–29).

Against Ham: Slavery, segregation, and racism sought to keep Ham under an eternal curse, even though Christ redeemed us from the curse by becoming a curse for us (Galatians 3:13).

Through Japheth, Satan distorted Japheth's enlargement into domination, conquest, and empire. Rather than dwelling in Shem's tents in humility, Japheth sought to displace Shem and enslave Ham.

Modern racial systems thus represent more than sociopolitical structures; they are spiritual strategies of division, designed to invert God's order and weaponize human difference against God's purposes.

Prophetic Witness and Biblical Mandate

The prophetic Scriptures reveal God's intention from the beginning: *"My house shall be called a house of prayer for all peoples"* (Isaiah 56:7). The early church glimpsed this in Cornelius (Acts 10), the Ethiopian eunuch (Acts 8), and the multiethnic church at Antioch (Acts 13:1–3). The final vision of Scripture is clear: a multitude no one can number, from every nation, tribe, people, and language, gathered before the Lamb (Revelation 7:9).

Thus, the church's historic complicity in systems of racial bigotry is a profound betrayal of its own eschatological identity. As Miroslav Volf argues, exclusion and domination are contradictions of the gospel, which calls us into embrace across lines of difference (Volf 1996, 66–70). The Catholic and Reformed churches tragically missed their cue. Instead of resisting Satan's jealous distortion of Japheth's destiny, they baptized it in law, liturgy, and doctrine. Instead of defending Shem and redeeming Ham, they sanctioned conquest and enslavement. Yet Scripture still calls the people of God to expose this demonic system, repent of complicity, and live into the multiethnic covenant reality of Christ's kingdom.

Bigotry as a Weaponized System: A Theological and Historical Analysis

Bigotry is not merely an attitude of the heart; it is a weaponized system, designed by the enemy to fracture humanity and subvert God's covenantal plan. Prejudice, the precursor to bigotry, is a pre-judgment— an opinion formed about someone before truly knowing them. The word derives from the Latin *prae* ("before") and *judicium* ("judgment"), reflecting humanity's proclivity to make assumptions without knowledge. Sin produces division, and Scripture shows us how jealousy and rivalry have existed since the earliest chapters of Genesis. Cain turned against Abel out of envy,^1 Ishmael and Isaac were set in tension,^2 and Jacob wrestled with Esau.^3 These conflicts illustrate how human brokenness manifests as hostility, often institutionalized over time.

Bigotry elevates prejudice into structural oppression. It is prejudice hardened into law, doctrine, and social custom. James Cone observes that "sin is the creation of situations in which people are oppressed," demonstrating that these divisions are neither accidental nor incidental but actively constructed (*God of the Oppressed* 153). Modern racial hierarchies, for instance, were deliberately engineered. Papal bulls such as *Dum Diversas* (1452), *Romanus Pontifex* (1455), and *Inter Caetera* (1493) authorized European powers to conquer, enslave, and dispossess non-Christian peoples.^4 Colonial laws, including seventeenth-century Virginia statutes, codified "whiteness" as a legal category, separating Europeans from Africans and Indigenous peoples.^5 By the eighteenth century, scientific racism claimed that Europeans were biologically superior, lending pseudo-scientific legitimacy to systemic oppression.^6

Underlying this construction is a spirit of jealousy, directed especially toward Shem. Through Shem's line came Israel, the covenant bearers, and ultimately Jesus, the Messiah (Genesis 12:1–3; Romans 9:4–5).^7 Salvation and covenant blessings are mediated through Shem, and Japheth, though promised enlargement, must receive through Shem rather than bypass him (Genesis 9:27).^8 Satan whispered rivalry into Japheth's descendants, just as he did to Cain against Abel and Esau against Jacob: *"If I cannot have the blessing, I will destroy the one who does."* This jealousy also targeted Ham, whose descendants were subjected to slavery, segregation, and systemic suppression despite the fact that the curse fell specifically on Canaan (Genesis 9:25).^9 Scholars such as J. Kameron Carter note that Western identity was historically constructed "over against the Jew," institutionalizing hostility toward Shem (*Race: A Theological Account* 34–36). Similarly, Esau McCaulley emphasizes that racist misreadings of Scripture have distorted God's intentions regarding Ham's descendants, when in Christ all curses are broken (*Reading While Black* 41–43).

Bigotry manifests in three overlapping forms: anti-Semitism, anti-Black racism, and white supremacy. Anti-Semitism has attempted to erase Shem's line through pogroms, the Inquisition, and the Holocaust.^10 Anti-Black racism demonized Ham's descendants, falsely claiming a curse and inferiority to justify slavery and oppression.^11 White supremacy elevated Japheth's descendants into godlike status, directly opposing the Kingdom of Christ. Kelly Brown Douglas observes that whiteness became a "sacred symbol of superiority" within Western Christianity, a counterfeit idol that structured social life (*Stand Your Ground* 12).

Yet redemption is possible. Japheth, historically the architect of much modern bigotry, is grafted into Shem's olive tree by faith in Christ (Romans 11:17–18).^12 Genesis 9:27's prophecy—that Japheth shall dwell in Shem's tents—is fulfilled not through domination but through the Gospel, which reconciles Jew and Gentile, slave and free, male and female (Galatians 3:28; Ephesians 2:11–14).^13 True repentance requires humility, renunciation of pride, and the embrace of covenantal unity. Jennings describes the necessity of repenting from "racial faith" to rediscover identity as guests at Israel's table (*The Christian Imagination* 289).

Resisting bigotry requires a reorientation toward God, His Kingdom, and His plan for humanity. Flesh and blood are not the enemy; principalities and powers are (Ephesians 6:12).^14 Humanity's diversity—nations, tribes, and tongues—is a gift, not a threat (Genesis 10; Revelation 7:9).^15 Jealousy, rivalry, and supremacy must be renounced, and Japheth must dwell in Shem's tents, not dominate them. As Miroslav Volf asserts, reconciliation, not exclusion, is the faithful human response: "There can be no future without embrace" (*Exclusion and Embrace* 29).

The church, historically complicit, now carries the prophetic task of resisting this evil. Where early Catholic and Reformed traditions failed, contemporary believers are called to expose, repent, and dismantle systems of bigotry. In Christ, Shem's covenant is secure, Ham is redeemed, and Japheth's blessing is fulfilled through humility and unity. The Kingdom of God summons humanity into reconciliation, gathered from every tribe and tongue before the Lamb (Revelation 7:9), declaring that no hierarchy of race or supremacy can stand in God's design.

Hidden Currents: *Racism, Spiritual Forces, and the Kingdom of God*

Most bigots are not consciously thinking about Christ. Many do not recognize the spiritual forces that shape their hearts, nor the historical and structural realities that undergird their actions. Yet their words and deeds still wield the destructive power of racism. This is because the system itself is larger than any one individual. Racism is not merely personal prejudice; it is a spiritual and structural reality, a hidden current running beneath the surface of society, shaping policies, behaviors, and attitudes—even when people cannot see it or refuse to acknowledge it.

From a Kingdom perspective, this is precisely why Jesus came: to confront the hidden works of darkness and to inaugurate a new way of life. The gospel exposes injustice and division, offering a vision for a society reordered by grace, mercy, and reconciliation. In John 8:32, Jesus said, *"You will know the truth, and the truth will set you free."* The truth of the Kingdom penetrates the unseen currents of oppression, liberating both hearts and structures from the power of sin.

Historically, these hidden currents have had devastating effects. The Transatlantic Slave Trade, colonialism, Jim Crow laws, and segregation were not merely the product of individual prejudice—they were the crystallization of systems built on fear, pride, and the misuse of Scripture, including the false Hamitic Hypothesis (Goldenberg 171; Sanders 98). Even after slavery ended, structural mechanisms— redlining, inequitable education, discriminatory insurance policies, and mass incarceration—continued to enforce the hidden currents of racial division. As Michelle Alexander notes, these systems operate "like a new caste system" in modern America, shaping life chances and perpetuating inequality long after the laws of segregation were abolished (Alexander 12).

Yet the Kingdom of God provides a counter-current, a deeper reality that reshapes hearts, communities, and nations. Christ calls His followers to engage both personally and structurally. Individually, believers are invited to repentance, humility, and the pursuit of justice (Micah 6:8). Collectively, the Church is called to dismantle the walls of oppression and to live as a prophetic witness to God's inclusive vision. Paul describes this Kingdom work in Ephesians 2:14–16: Christ has broken down the dividing wall of hostility, reconciling Jew and Gentile into one new humanity. In this reconciliation, the Church models a society that reflects God's justice and mercy, challenging every hidden current of division.

The spiritual dimension of racism cannot be overstated. Satan has always sought to exploit pride, fear, and resentment to fracture the human family. From Genesis 3, where disobedience brought separation from God, to Cain's murder of Abel in Genesis 4, to the scattering at Babel in Genesis 11, the enemy's strategy has been consistent: divide humanity and obscure God's plan of redemption. These ancient patterns echo today in systems and structures that perpetuate inequality, whether economic, cultural, or educational.

For people of color, this is painfully evident. Anger, resentment, and pride are often not sins invented by individuals but consequences of living under a system designed to oppress. Yet the gospel provides the antidote. Jesus unites all humanity in Himself, reconciling Jew and Gentile, rich and poor, Black, Brown, and White, into a single covenantal family. This reconciliation is both spiritual and practical: it transforms hearts, restores relationships, and challenges structures of oppression.

In my own life, I have witnessed the corrosive power of these hidden currents, from childhood experiences with discriminatory insurance policies to encounters with systemic racism in schools and communities. Yet I have also seen the transformative power of Christ's Kingdom. Where pride and resentment once ruled, Christ plants forgiveness. Where anger and exclusion once festered, He creates unity. And where systems of oppression have hardened hearts, His Spirit softens them, drawing every tribe and nation into covenantal inclusion.

The Kingdom of God is not passive; it is a living, active force that calls His Church to action. To confront racism is not merely to oppose bad behavior—it is to dismantle structures, challenge hidden currents, and proclaim the truth that every life is sacred, every person is valued, and every nation is welcome in the family of God. As Revelation 7:9 proclaims, the ultimate vision of the Kingdom is a multitude "from every nation, tribe, people and language, standing before the throne and before the Lamb," worshiping together in unity. This is the promise, the hope, and the calling of every believer: to bring the invisible Kingdom of God into the visible world, dismantling the hidden currents of division and building a society that reflects God's covenantal love.

Racism is Systemic and Not Just Personal Hate

Many people assume that racism only exists when someone utters a slur or harbors open hatred toward another group. But the truth is far deeper. Racism is not just a collection of individual acts—it is a constructed system, a hidden current that has flowed through societies long before most of us were born. It operates quietly, yet powerfully, through laws, economics, education, and culture, shaping the opportunities and outcomes of entire communities.

Even those who bear no personal ill will can perpetuate its effects simply by participating in the structures of society as they exist. But the Kingdom of God calls us to something radically different. Christ does not leave us passive within these currents; He calls us to discern them, confront them, and help reorder the world according to His justice and mercy. In the Kingdom, every law, every system, every institution is invited to reflect God's heart for equality, inclusion, and the inherent dignity of every person.

Racism is not just a human problem—it is a spiritual one, a distortion of God's creation and covenant. And yet, in Christ, the hidden currents of oppression can be exposed and overturned, as His Kingdom breaks through every system that seeks to divide and diminish humanity. A banker may not personally hate anyone, but if the policies he follows deny loans to certain neighborhoods (redlining), he is still enforcing racism — whether he realizes it or not. The Bible shows us that evil spiritual powers work through human systems:

Ephesians 6:12 *"For we wrestle not against flesh and blood, but against principalities, against powers, against the rulers of the darkness of this world, against spiritual wickedness in high places."*

Racism as a Spiritual and Structural Reality: *The Kingdom's Response*

Racism is far more than personal prejudice or bad ideas—it is a spiritual and systemic force. Rooted in the enemy's strategy to divide humanity, it manifests in ways both visible and invisible. As Ephesians 6:12 warns, "For our struggle is not against flesh and blood, but against the rulers, against the authorities, against the powers of this dark world and against the spiritual forces of evil in the heavenly realms." These spiritual forces embed themselves into structures: governments, economies, educational systems, and cultural norms, shaping society's patterns and creating hidden currents of oppression.

Even those who bear no personal malice can perpetuate this system because the currents of sin are bigger than any single individual. The enemy uses human pride, fear, and ignorance as tools, moving through individuals like instruments—often unconsciously—to advance division and injustice. Historically, we see this in slavery, segregation, colonialism, and discriminatory laws and policies. Systems like redlining, unequal educational funding, and discriminatory insurance policies persisted long after the moral failures of individuals were exposed, demonstrating that racism operates structurally as well as personally (Alexander 12; Goldenberg 171).

The Kingdom of God, however, offers a radically different reality. Christ's mission is to expose, confront, and dismantle these forces. Where Satan seeks division, Jesus calls for reconciliation; where he sows resentment, Christ pours the living water of forgiveness and unity. Galatians 3:28 reminds us: *"There is neither Jew nor Greek, slave nor free, male nor female, for you are all one in Christ Jesus."* In the Kingdom, no structural or spiritual force is beyond the reach of God's redeeming power.

Jesus' redemptive work is both personal and societal. Individually, He transforms hearts, freeing believers from the chains of anger, pride, and

100

prejudice. Collectively, the Church is called to be an instrument of justice and reconciliation. Miroslav Volf notes that God's Kingdom is built on embrace and reconciliation, rather than domination or exclusion: "To be embraced is to be included in the community that mirrors God's own self-giving love, and exclusion is the antithesis of this divine vision" (Volf 55). Through Christ, every ethnic group, tribe, and nation can be brought together under one covenantal family, embodying the Kingdom on earth as it is in heaven.

Historically, failure to embrace this Kingdom vision has caused immense suffering. Racism justified slavery, oppression, and segregation by distorting Scripture and misappropriating theological ideas such as the Hamitic Hypothesis or pseudoscientific claims of racial hierarchy (Goldenberg 171; Sanders 521). Even in contemporary society, systems of inequality—whether economic, educational, or legal—can perpetuate the hidden currents of division, demonstrating the continuing influence of spiritual and structural forces aligned against God's Kingdom.

Yet Christ's victory offers hope and power. In Him, the Church is called to discern these currents, resist the enemy's schemes, and actively pursue reconciliation and justice. As Paul exhorts in Ephesians 2:14–16, Jesus "has broken down the dividing wall of hostility" and created one new humanity. The Kingdom of God calls believers to participate in that reconciliation, transforming not only hearts but institutions, policies, and cultures.

In practice, this means actively confronting systems of oppression, speaking truth to power, and embodying the radical inclusion of the gospel. It means challenging racism wherever it exists—in laws, in schools, in communities—and modeling a society reordered under Christ's authority. The Kingdom is not theoretical; it is lived, breathed, and enacted in acts of justice, mercy, and love that restore human dignity.

Ultimately, racism is both a spiritual and structural reality, but it is not invincible. Christ's Kingdom is greater, His power unstoppable, and His vision for humanity unifying. Where Satan seeks to divide, Christ unites; where the enemy sows fear, Christ pours love; and where systems of oppression entrench injustice, the Kingdom offers liberation. Believers are called to step into this mission, discerning, resisting, and transforming the world as instruments of God's redemptive plan.

Why Japheth's Descendants Wield Ideology So Powerfully

Historically, Europeans (Japheth's line) created and globalized this system through colonialism, slavery, and white supremacy. They constructed racial categories to justify conquest and exploitation. They embedded these ideas in laws, education, and economics, making them self-perpetuating.

Even today, many who wield this power did not design it — they inherited   it.
However, inherited power still functions spiritually, whether or not someone consciously chooses it. A person born into a house with poisoned water may not have poisoned it, but if they drink it and serve it to others, the poison still spreads.

The System of Bigotry and the Kingdom Response

Bigotry is more than personal prejudice; it is a weaponized system embedded deeply in global society. It perpetuates itself, even among those who do not consciously identify as racist. The system operates through multiple channels. Education, for instance, often distorts or erases historical truths, sanitizing oppression and marginalizing the experiences of Shem's and Ham's descendants. Economics channels advantage to certain groups through policies that maintain generational wealth disparities. Religion can become complicit when theologies either justify oppression or adopt a false "color-blindness" that ignores systemic sin. Politics, too, codifies inequity through laws that appear neutral but in practice reinforce existing hierarchies. These structures are so embedded that they seem to have lives of their own. As James Cone notes, sin is "structural as well as personal," and the systems of oppression endure because many simply participate, whether knowingly or unwittingly (*God of the Oppressed* 153).

This reality is why the fight against bigotry cannot focus solely on individual attitudes. Ephesians 6:12 reminds believers: *"For we wrestle not against flesh and blood, but against the rulers, against the authorities, against the cosmic powers over this present darkness, against the spiritual forces of evil in the heavenly places."* The principalities use both the individual and the system to attack God's covenantal plan for Shem, Ham, and Japheth. A bigot may act out of fear, pride, or hatred, yet in doing so, they operate within a system designed centuries ago to perpetuate racial hierarchy and injustice. The system is like a weapon already loaded; anyone who picks it up wields demonic power, whether they recognize it or not.

Yet the gospel offers a counter-weapon. The Kingdom of God has the authority to dismantle these structures, heal wounds, and restore God's intended order. Jesus breaks the power of systemic sin, but this requires three interrelated responses from His people. First is exposure: bringing hidden structures of injustice into the light. John 3:19–21 demonstrates this principle, showing that light exposes what is hidden and convicts hearts. Second is repentance: both individuals and nations must turn from pride, domination, and the false sense of superiority that fuels structural oppression (Acts 17:30). Third is Kingdom identity: believers walk in Christ's authority to confront powers, not just people. Ephesians 2:14–16 declares: *"For He Himself is our peace, who has made the two groups one and has destroyed the barrier, the dividing wall of hostility..."* The Kingdom's response is to recognize that the fight is not merely against flesh and blood but against a principality using human instruments to enforce division.

Christ's mission embodies this Kingdom response. Luke 4:18 recounts Him proclaiming: *"He has sent me to proclaim freedom for the captives and recovery of sight for the blind, to set the oppressed free."* This includes those blinded by hatred itself, whether through internalized prejudice or systemic conditioning. The Kingdom of God wields truth to expose lies of racial hierarchy, love to heal wounds of division, and spiritual authority to break the strongholds over both people and structures. Scholars such as Willie James Jennings and Miroslav Volf emphasize that reconciliation is a radical, systemic project: it requires transforming both hearts and societal frameworks (*The Christian Imagination* 289; *Exclusion and Embrace* 29).

Ultimately, resisting racialized bigotry requires discernment and courage. The system operates independently of conscious intention, yet the Kingdom calls believers to act decisively. By exposing injustice, repenting from complicity, and exercising Christ's authority, the church participates in dismantling structures that have opposed God's plan for Shem, Ham, and Japheth for centuries. Where Satan weaponized division, Christ brings reconciliation; where human systems enforced hierarchy, God calls His people to embody unity. The gospel is both personal and systemic, illuminating the hearts of individuals while dismantling the powers that maintain oppression.

Privilege, Biblical History and the Kingdom of God

The question of racial hierarchy and privilege is not a modern invention. While some deny the existence of "white privilege" in contemporary society, biblical history demonstrates the roots and consequences of systemic inequality. God's Word shows a pattern in which humanity, through jealousy and sin, established hierarchies that distorted His design for Shem, Ham, and Japheth. Japheth's descendants, historically empowered to dominate through the construction of racial systems, must now repent because the Kingdom of God is at hand (Genesis 9:27; Romans 11:17–18).

White privilege, as sociologist Peggy McIntosh has observed, is an "invisible knapsack" of advantages embedded within social structures, allowing some groups to prosper at the expense of others.^1 This contemporary sociological insight mirrors what Scripture demonstrates: human systems, when left unchecked, become tools of oppression. Ham's descendants were enslaved, Shem's descendants were persecuted, and Japheth's descendants built empires that elevated themselves over both. The pattern is unmistakable in history, from colonial expansion sanctioned by papal authority (*Dum Diversas, Romanus Pontifex, Inter Caetera*) to the racialized legal codes of early America.^2

Scripture frames the remedy and the hope in terms of the Kingdom of God. The fall of Adam brought consequences for all humanity (Genesis 3:16–19), and in some sense, God permitted these inequalities to unfold within the temporal order. Yet the advent of Christ inaugurates a new epoch in which the sons of God rise, and His Kingdom begins to displace human hierarchies (Matthew 5:3–10; Luke 4:18). Paul makes it explicit: Gentiles, Japheth's descendants, are grafted into Israel's olive tree by faith in Christ (Romans 11:17–18), and all divisions are overcome in the reconciliation of Jew and Gentile (Ephesians 2:14–16; Galatians 3:28).^3

Dispensationalist theology, with its tendency to separate the modern church from God's ongoing covenant with Israel, provides no escape from this reality. Israel's hope is inseparable from the Kingdom of God, especially as prophetic events unfold toward the tribulation. As contemporary observers note, the tribulation is not solely a future event but manifests in current global crises, including systemic oppression, racial injustice, and the exploitation of marginalized peoples (Revelation 6:5–8). The church cannot evade its calling; God is fulfilling something special for Israel, and the Kingdom must be made manifest now.

Thus, repentance is the only path forward for Japheth and all who have benefited from privilege. Kingdom identity requires humility, exposure of systemic sin, and active participation in dismantling structures that oppose God's design (John 3:19–21; Acts 17:30). Christ's authority is the means by which believers confront principalities, not just individual sinners (Ephesians 6:12). This is not merely ethical exhortation; it is prophetic necessity. Jennings and Volf emphasize that racial reconciliation is systemic, requiring both structural transformation and the renewal of the human imagination in line with God's covenantal purposes (*The Christian Imagination* 289; *Exclusion and Embrace* 29).

To resist white privilege and racialized power structures, the church must act decisively. It must recognize that the fight is not against individuals alone but against entrenched spiritual and social forces. Bigotry, when left unchecked, becomes a self-perpetuating system; only the Kingdom of God, empowered by Christ and manifested through His followers, can dismantle it. Japheth's repentance is part of a broader divine mandate: to dwell in Shem's tents, honor God's covenant with Ham, and allow the Kingdom to fully displace human hierarchies. The time is now. There is no escape; the Kingdom of God is imminent, and all who bear the name of Christ must rise to their calling.

A Message from the Heart

Intelligence is the ability to learn, reason, solve problems, and make decisions. In chess, we think several moves ahead; similarly, the discoveries I present here are data-driven and grounded in credible research.

Accepting these conclusions has been difficult. In many ways, I have wrestled with them my whole life. What I describe is, in effect, a human-made system that attempts to replicate certain functions of natural intelligence. I have a profound faith in God and in the message of the Kingdom, and the recent years — from conflicts with law enforcement and the deaths of George Floyd and Trayvon Martin, to the January 6th insurrection and other political upheavals — have deeply affected me and helped inspire this book.

From the perspective of the Kingdom of God, true life and spiritual intelligence flow from our spirit and are processed through our soul-mind. They are revealed and breathed into us by God (Genesis 2:7). This revelation on racism and its subsequent effects on all of humanity was not something I sought - it was given. I do not claim special cleverness or wish to impress anyone. I reject the harm that the constructs of race, prejudice, and discrimination have done, and the source of my understanding — shaped and confirmed by historical data — is God Himself. He breathed this understanding into me, connecting my living spirit to my soul-mind; touching my consciousness, self-awareness, emotions, and moral sense, and prompting me, by free will, to share it with you.

Imagination opens new worlds of understanding, and the Lord empowers us to love purely. I wish the world were different, and I would have never had to grapple with these issues all of my life. That is why I am promoting the Kingdom of God so passionately; because, within it, the divisions that scar us vanish, and every person is free to form relationships rooted in love, empathy, and spiritual connection.

I have examined a large body of real data — data that is accurate, verified, and complete. There are many competing theories about the origin of race, racism, prejudice, and discrimination, and people propagate these ideas every day. True wisdom and discernment come from the Spirit of God, who, if we ask, will guide our decisions in the right direction (James 1:5; Proverbs 2:6). Human sin and pride corrupted what was meant to be good. Misreadings of Scripture and distorted tradition fashioned systems apart from God's purposes, rather than reflecting righteousness, love, and justice.

The Bible presents genealogies as a theological and literary framework — a way of showing identity and relationship within God's unfolding plan for humanity — not as a scientific account of race. Early interpreters, both Jewish and Christian, and later European writers, sometimes mapped these names onto historical peoples and used those mappings to justify ideas about lineage and superiority *(for example, applying labels like "Japhethites" to Europeans)*. But the genealogies are better understood as symbolic representations of cultural, linguistic, and political ties than as biological or anthropological categories.

Today, "race" is studied biologically, anthropologically, and genetically — and the evidence shows that human beings share far more in common than simple genealogical labels suggest. From the perspective of the Kingdom of God, Scripture's genealogies affirm a common origin in Adam and call us to unity. They do not teach that some races possess greater worth or dignity. Instead, they reveal a diverse human family with a moral and redemptive purpose that transcends ethnicity.

The misinterpretation of Genesis 9 — the so-called "Hamitic hypothesis" and the perverse "curse of Ham" rationale — represents a tragic distortion of Scripture that fueled systems of supremacy. Those readings are not faithful to God's ultimate purpose - the expansion of His Kingdom that values every person equally.

This book is my attempt to speak plainly about these things - to bring together spiritual insight and careful research, to lament the harms done by prejudice, and to point toward a Kingdom vision where love, justice, and unity prevail. If the Spirit of God grants wisdom, may these pages help guide us into greater truth and reconciliation.

The story in Genesis 9:20–27 begins right after the flood, when Noah starts life again as a man of the soil. He plants a vineyard, harvests its grapes, and makes wine. One day, he drinks too much, becomes drunk, and lies uncovered inside his tent.

Ham, one of Noah's sons, comes across his father's nakedness. Instead of keeping the matter private, he goes and tells his brothers, Shem and Japheth. They respond differently. Taking a garment, they walk backward into the tent so they will not see their father exposed, and they gently cover him.

When Noah wakes up and realizes what has happened, he pronounces a curse and a blessing. But notice carefully: the curse is spoken over Canaan, Ham's son — not Ham himself, not all of Ham's children, and certainly not all nations. Noah says, "Cursed be Canaan; a servant of servants shall he be to his brothers." Meanwhile, Shem and Japheth are blessed for their act of honor.

That is what the text actually says. There is no mention of race, skin color, or any curse passed down to all of Ham's descendants. Yet, over time, this passage was twisted and misused to build what became known as the Hamitic hypothesis — a distorted teaching that fueled prejudice and even justified slavery.

Here's how the distortion spread:

People confused Canaan with all of Ham's descendants, stretching a single curse into one that supposedly covered entire peoples, especially those who were not white.

They added details that aren't there — claiming that Ham's name meant "dark" or "black," and from that, teaching that dark skin was somehow part of the curse. But the Hebrew text never says this.

The curse was then weaponized. In the American South before the Civil War, preachers and politicians pointed to this story as proof that African slavery was divinely ordained. It was a social and political misuse of Scripture, not God's truth.

Some scholars even suggest that the way the genealogies were shaped over time may reflect later edits or emphases, influenced by cultural or theological agendas.

The heartbreaking result is that a story about respect and dishonor within one family was twisted into a justification for racism and oppression. Instead of reflecting God's justice and love, it became a tool of division.

There is no strong textual basis for race or color being part of the curse. The original Hebrew doesn't allude to skin color as part of the curse. It is an added interpretation. Much of the hypothesis comes from later traditions, cultural assumptions, and fear/prejudice, not from sound biblical exegesis.

Scripture teaches that all humans are made in God's image (Genesis 1:27). Any ideology that claims one group is "cursed" permanently because of race conflicts with the biblical teaching of equality in dignity and redemption. Modern biblical scholarship generally rejects the use of Genesis 9 as a support for race-based inferiority or as a justification for slavery or eternal servitude based on race. The "Hamitic hypothesis" is viewed as a corruption of biblical text to serve social and political purposes.

In the Kingdom of God, every single person carries immeasurable worth because each of us is created in the image of God. No son or daughter of Ham—or of any family line—is less human, less loved, or less valuable. At the cross of Christ, every curse is broken. Through Him, we are welcomed as sons and daughters of God, citizens of His Kingdom, and heirs of a new covenant that transcends old divisions and destroys barriers of race, status, or heritage.

This is why we must handle Scripture with reverence and care. When it is misread or misused, it can become a weapon of injustice and even sin. Tragically, that is what happened with Genesis 9. The text never teaches that Ham's descendants are cursed because of skin color or race. The so-called Hamitic hypothesis was a distortion of the Word of God—twisted by human pride and prejudice to defend slavery, racism, and colonialism.

The truth of Genesis is far more precise and far more hopeful - the curse pronounced there was directed at Canaan, the son of Ham—not at Ham himself or all of his children; and certainly not at whole groups of people based on color. To turn this into a theology of racial hierarchy is to misrepresent God's Word and misjudge His heart.

In God's Kingdom, the story is not one of division but of redemption. Christ Himself tears down the walls we build and restores the dignity of every image-bearer, calling us into one family united in love, justice, and grace.

The Bottom Line

What I have shared here is both trustworthy and rooted in the truth of Scripture. The so-called Hamitic hypothesis, along with many other racial claims born in later centuries, is not reliable. These ideas are the result of misreading the Bible, fueled by cultural bias and social misuse—not by the Word of God itself.

God's Word remains pure, authoritative, and unchanging, even when human beings have twisted it for their own purposes. Though Scripture was misapplied to justify slavery and racial hierarchy, its original intent has always stood firm. During the transatlantic slave trade and European colonial expansion, this distorted interpretation of Genesis 9 was tragically used in sermons, legal systems, and academic texts to rationalize slavery and oppression. Historians confirm this pattern:

Britannica notes that "the Hamitic hypothesis was used to explain the origin of African civilizations and to justify European domination of African peoples."

MDPI research demonstrates how the so-called "curse of Ham" was repeatedly invoked to legitimize slavery and racial oppression.

But the Kingdom of God holds fast to a higher truth - the Word of God is trustworthy. As followers of Christ, we must acknowledge that Scripture can be twisted for evil purposes (James 3:1–6). Recognizing this helps us separate human distortion from divine revelation, guarding both ourselves and our world from misuse in social, cultural, or political contexts.

At its heart, Scripture upholds the unity and dignity of all people. From the very beginning, we are told that every human being is made in God's image (Genesis 1:27), and Paul affirms that all nations come from one blood (Acts 17:26). There is no biblical warrant for racial hierarchy—only a call to love, justice, and reconciliation in Christ.

May we, with humility and courage, read God's Word faithfully, reject distortions, and bear witness to the Kingdom where every person is valued, every barrier is broken, and Christ is all in all.

Epilogue

America's Greatness Through the Lens of God's Kingdom

"When was America great?" This question forces us to confront both historical reality and moral imagination. If greatness is measured by military might, economic output, or technological achievement, one might point to the industrial age, global innovation, or even the post-World War II era. Yet, viewed through the lens of God's Kingdom, greatness is measured not by dominance but by righteousness, justice, mercy, and service (Matthew 20:26; Micah 6:8). From this perspective, much of American history reveals both promise and failure—*a nation of potential often undercut by systemic oppression, exploitation, and moral compromise.*

The Declaration of Independence (1776) boldly proclaimed that *"all men are created equal"*. This revolutionary vision articulated a Kingdom-aligned ideal - God's image is present in all people, and liberty and dignity are universal. Yet reality diverged sharply from principle. Slavery remained legal, women could not vote, and Indigenous peoples were violently displaced (Saunt 2014). In the new nation, America's "greatness" was aspirational—an expression of potential rather than practice.

The Post–Civil War Era offered a brief glimpse of transformative justice. The abolition of slavery through the 13th Amendment, the political participation of African Americans, and the establishment of Black churches and schools reflected Kingdom values: *justice, restoration, and communal flourishing* (Alexander 2010; Cone 1969). Yet Reconstruction was violently suppressed. Jim Crow laws, lynching, and systemic disenfranchisement reversed much of this progress, demonstrating that structural injustice resists simple moral progress.

Industrial Expansion and Economic Growth in the late 19th and early 20th centuries produced material wealth, but often at tremendous human cost. Exploitation of child labor, wage theft, unsafe working conditions, and racialized segregation meant that technological or economic achievement could not equate to spiritual or ethical greatness (Proverbs 14:34; Feagin 2020). Indeed, the spiritual condition of the nation often contradicted its material ambitions. True Kingdom greatness emerges not from power amassed or wealth accumulated, but from the flourishing of human dignity and the embodiment of justice (Matthew 5:3; Luke 4:18).

People of Color: *African Americans, Indigenous peoples, Asian Americans, and Latinos* have consistently borne the weight of oppression while simultaneously embodying Kingdom principles through resilience, creativity, and faith. Enslaved Africans sustained spiritual life through song, prayer, and communal worship, planting seeds of liberation theology that would flourish in the Black church (Cone 2011; Baldwin 1993). Indigenous peoples resisted dispossession, preserving spiritual and cultural knowledge despite forced relocation, massacres, and assimilation policies such as boarding schools (Painter 2010; Precept Austin 2025). Asian and Latino communities contributed labor, commerce, and culture, often under duress and facing systemic discrimination, from the Chinese Exclusion Act to wage theft and land dispossession (Bonilla-Silva 2022; Feagin 2020).

The Civil Rights Movement (1950s–1960s) exemplifies the closest America has come to Kingdom greatness. African American leaders such as Dr. Martin Luther King Jr., Rosa Parks, and Malcolm X, alongside countless unnamed activists, embodied servant leadership, courage, and prophetic vision. They confronted systemic racism, organized communities around the principles of justice, mercy, and reconciliation, and leveraged faith as both moral and strategic authority (King 1963; King 1967). Indigenous movements like AIM, Latino labor organizers like César Chávez and Dolores Huerta, and Asian American activists collectively advanced justice in alignment with biblical imperatives (Micah 6:8).

Yet, even as these communities demonstrated Kingdom principles, structural inequities persisted. Mass incarceration, poverty, health disparities, and anti-Asian violence reveal that systemic injustice is enduring and often adaptive (Alexander 2010; JustFaith Ministries 2023). America's material achievements have rarely translated into moral or spiritual completeness. As Mark 8:36 warns, *"For what shall it profit a man, if he shall gain the whole world, and lose his own soul?"*

Kingdom truth reframes greatness entirely. For white America, historical "greatness" often meant privilege, dominance, or the accumulation of power. For people of color, true greatness has always been spiritual, manifest in faith, resistance, creativity, and communal endurance under persecution. Like the early church under Roman oppression, marginalized communities carried the Cross while building Kingdom outposts—churches, schools, cultural institutions—that embodied God's justice and mercy before the wider society acknowledged them (Cone 1970; Douglas 2015).

America can only be truly great when it aligns with Kingdom principles: serving the vulnerable, advancing justice, and honoring God's design for human dignity. Matthew 20:26 reminds us, *"Whoever wants to become great among you must be your servant."* Greatness is realized not in dominance or wealth, but in sacrificial love, prophetic witness, and faithful obedience to God. Communities that have borne oppression have, paradoxically, provided the clearest vision of Kingdom greatness, offering the wider nation a blueprint for justice, mercy, and reconciliation.

The Church is called to embody this vision, to act as both conscience and corrective. Kingdom spaces—faith communities committed to equity, worship, prophetic witness, and social transformation—reveal glimpses of God's justice breaking into a fractured society (Volf 1996; Edmondson & Brennan 2022). The Spirit moves in these spaces, turning sorrow into hope, oppression into resilience, and trial into triumph.

America's true greatness has always been hidden in the very communities it tried to erase. African Americans, Indigenous peoples, Asians, Latinos, and other marginalized communities have lived out the principles of God's Kingdom, often at great personal cost, demonstrating that service, mercy, and justice are the metrics of true greatness. It is these communities, faithfully bearing the weight of God's Kingdom, that hold the key to the nation's redemption.

Brothers and sisters, the call is clear. The Kingdom is here, and it is now. America will only truly shine when it repents, serves, and elevates righteousness over privilege. The Church, empowered by Christ, must rise to the challenge, modeling Kingdom leadership, love, and justice in every sphere of life. The time has come to move from aspiration to action, from hypocrisy to holiness, from oppression to the realization of God's design. True greatness is not a relic of the past—it is present wherever the Kingdom manifests, and it is calling us to embody it faithfully, courageously, and boldly.

The Kingdom is here and the Kingdom is now.

Works Cited

Key Scholarly Sources

Scholar / Work	Key Insights Relevant to This Statement
The Forging of Races: Race and Scripture in the Protestant Atlantic World, 1600-2000 (Cambridge)	This work shows how European Christians used interpretations of Genesis and other biblical texts to construct ideas of race; it argues that "race-as-theology" has been central in European colonial thought. Cambridge University Press & Assessment
"Race and Ethnicity in the New Testament" **(Bible Odyssey)**	Discusses how terms like *ethnos*, *genos*, *laos*, etc., are more about people groups, tribes, or nations rather than modern racial categories; emphasizes that New Testament identity is inclusive rather than dividive. zondervanacademic.bibleodyssey.com
Christian Research Institute, "Putting Race in Biblical Perspective"	Affirms that all humanity is from one ancestor (Adam) and that race, as used in modern contexts, is a social construct; uses biblical passages to show that divisions based on race are contrary to the Gospel. Equip

Bibliography

Primary Sources

- **The Babylonian Talmud.** *Sanhedrin 70a.* Translated by Isidore Epstein, Soncino Press, 1935. (×1)
- **The Holy Bible, New International Version.** Zondervan, 2011. (×9)
- **"Dum Diversas."** 18 June 1452. Papal Encyclicals Online / Unam Sanctam Catholicam. Accessed 23 Sept. 2025. (×7)
- **"Inter Caetera."** 4 May 1493. Papal Encyclicals Online / Encyclopedia Virginia. Accessed 23 Sept. 2025. (×7)
- **"Romanus Pontifex."** 1455. Papal Encyclicals Online / papalencyclicals.net. Accessed 23 Sept. 2025. (×7)
- **Geneva Study Bible.** "Commentary – Genesis 10." Christianity.com. Accessed 22 Sept. 2025. (×2)
- **Henry, Matthew.** "Commentary on Genesis 10." *Matthew Henry's Commentary on the Whole Bible: Old Testament*, St-Takla.org. Accessed 22 Sept. 2025. (×2)
- **Luther, Martin.** *On the Jews and Their Lies.* 1543. (×2)
- **Precept Austin.** "Genesis 10 Commentary." PreceptAustin.org. Accessed 22 Sept. 2025. (×3)
- **Rashi.** Commentary on Genesis 9:22. *Mikraot Gedolot.* (×1)
- **"An Act Concerning Servants and Slaves (1705)."** Encyclopedia Virginia, Virginia Foundation for the Humanities. Accessed 23 Sept. 2025. (×2)

Secondary Scholarship

- **Alexander, Michelle.** *The New Jim Crow: Mass Incarceration in the Age of Colorblindness.* The New Press, 2010. (×4)
- **Allen, Theodore W.** *The Invention of the White Race.* Verso, 1994–1997. (×2)
- **Appiah, Kwame Anthony.** *The Ethics of Identity.* Princeton UP, 2005. (×3)
- **Baldwin, James.** *The Fire Next Time.* Vintage International, 1993. (×3)

- **Bonilla-Silva, Eduardo.** *Racism Without Racists: Color-Blind Racism and the Persistence of Racial Inequality in America.* 6th ed., Rowman & Littlefield, 2022. (×3)
- **Brueggemann, Walter.** *Theology of the Old Testament: Testimony, Dispute, Advocacy.* Fortress Press, 1997. (×1)
- **Carter, J. Kameron.** *Race: A Theological Account.* Oxford University Press, 2008. (×8)
- **Cone, James H.** *A Black Theology of Liberation.* Orbis Books, 1970. (×2)
- **Cone, James H.** *Black Theology and Black Power.* Orbis Books, 1969. (×3)
- **Cone, James H.** *The Cross and the Lynching Tree.* Orbis Books, 2011. (×6)
- **Cone, James H.** *God of the Oppressed.* Orbis Books, 1997. (×6)
- **Douglas, Kelly Brown.** *Stand Your Ground: Black Bodies and the Justice of God.* Orbis Books, 2015. (×6)
- **Edmondson, Christina, and Chad Brennan.** *Faithful Antiracism: Moving Past Talk to Systemic Change.* IVP Academic, 2022. (×3)
- **Ehrman, Bart D.** *Jesus: Apocalyptic Prophet of the New Millennium.* Oxford University Press, 1999. (×3)
- **Feagin, Joe R.** *The White Racial Frame: Centuries of Racial Framing and Counter-Framing.* 3rd ed., Routledge, 2020. (×3)
- **Goldenberg, David M.** *The Curse of Ham: Race and Slavery in Early Judaism, Christianity, and Islam.* Princeton UP, 2003. (×3)
- **Gould, Stephen Jay.** *The Mismeasure of Man.* W. W. Norton, 1981. (×2)
- **Heen, Michael L.** "Insurance and Race." *Yale Journal on Regulation*, vol. 24, no. 2, 2007, pp. 389–445. (×3)
- **Heng, Geraldine.** *Empire of Magic: Medieval Romance and the Politics of Cultural Fantasy.* Columbia University Press, 2003. (×3)
- **Herrnstein, Richard J., and Charles Murray.** *The Bell Curve: Intelligence and Class Structure in American Life.* Free Press, 1994. (×2)
- **Jennings, Willie James.** *The Christian Imagination: Theology and the Origins of Race.* Yale University Press, 2010. (×9)
- **Jordan, Winthrop D.** *White Over Black: American Attitudes Toward the Negro, 1550–1812.* W. W. Norton, 1968. (×1)

- **JustFaith Ministries.** *Faith and Racial Justice: Changing Systems and Structures.* JustFaith, 2023. (×3)
- **Keller, Catherine.** *Face of the Deep: A Theology of Becoming.* Routledge, 2003. (×2)
- **Kendi, Ibram X.** *How to Be an Antiracist.* One World, 2019. (×2)
- **Kendi, Ibram X.** *Stamped from the Beginning: The Definitive History of Racist Ideas in America.* Nation Books, 2016. (×2)
- **Kerner Commission.** *Report of the National Advisory Commission on Civil Disorders.* U.S. Government Printing Office, 1968. (×1)
- **King, Martin Luther, Jr.** *Letter from Birmingham Jail.* 1963. Reprinted in *Why We Can't Wait*, Signet Classics, 2000, pp. 289–302. (×4)
- **King, Martin Luther, Jr.** *Where Do We Go from Here: Chaos or Community?* Harper & Row, 1967. (×3)
- **Levine, Amy-Jill.** *The Misunderstood Jew: The Church and the Scandal of the Jewish Jesus.* HarperOne, 2006. (×4)
- **McCaulley, Esau.** *Reading While Black: African American Biblical Interpretation as an Exercise in Hope.* IVP Academic, 2020. (×6)
- **McIntosh, Peggy.** "White Privilege: Unpacking the Invisible Knapsack." *Peace and Freedom*, 1989. (×3)
- **Miller, Patrick D.** *The History of Israelite Religion: Ancient Traditions in Context.* Fortress Press, 2000. (×2)
- **Orfield, Gary, and Chungmei Lee.** *Racial Transformation and the Changing Nature of Segregation.* Harvard Civil Rights Project, 2005. (×1)
- **Painter, Nell Irvin.** *The History of White People.* W. W. Norton, 2010. (×4)
- **Sanders, Edith R.** "The Hamitic Hypothesis: Its Origin and Functions in Time Perspective." *Journal of African History*, vol. 10, no. 4, 1969, pp. 521–532. (×3)
- **Saunt, Claudio.** *West of the Revolution: An Uncommon History of 1776.* W. W. Norton, 2014. (×2)
- **Schweikart, Larry.** *The Non-Business Side of Business History: Insurance, Actuarial Science, and Race.* Routledge, 2010. (×3)
- **Soulen, R. Kendall.** *The God of Israel and Christian Theology.* Fortress Press, 2008. (×2)

- **Sowell, Thomas.** *Race and Culture: A World View.* Basic Books, 1994. (×3)
- **Sugrue, Thomas J.** *Sweet Land of Liberty: The Forgotten Struggle for Civil Rights in the North.* Random House, 2008. (×2)
- **Volf, Miroslav.** *Exclusion and Embrace: A Theological Exploration of Identity, Otherness, and Reconciliation.* Abingdon Press, 1996. (×9)
- **Wilson, Jonathan.** "The White Jesus: Race, Art, and Theology in Early Modern Europe." *Journal of Religion and Culture*, vol. 27, no. 2, 2014, pp. 33–58. (×3)
- **Wright, N. T.** *Paul and the Faithfulness of God.* Fortress Press, 2013. (×2)

Scripture References

Genesis 9:20–27 – Noah's prophecy concerning Shem, Ham, and Japheth.

Genesis 10 – The Table of Nations, setting the framework for humanity's divisions.

Genesis 12:1–3 – The Abrahamic covenant and God's blessing through Shem's line.

Genesis 25:19–34 – Rivalry between Jacob and Esau as a paradigm of division and jealousy.

Exodus 1:8–14 – Israel oppressed in Egypt, foreshadowing systemic injustice.

Deuteronomy 10:17–19 – God shows no partiality and commands love for the stranger.

Psalm 133:1 – "How good and pleasant it is when God's people live together in unity!"

Proverbs 14:34 – "Righteousness exalts a nation, but sin condemns any people."

Isaiah 2:2–4 – Nations streaming to the mountain of the Lord for peace and justice.

Isaiah 56:6–8 – God's house as "a house of prayer for all nations."

Micah 6:8 – "What does the Lord require of you but to do justice, love mercy, and walk humbly with your God?"

Luke 4:18–19 – Jesus' mission: good news to the poor, freedom for the oppressed.

John 3:19–21 – The call to expose evil deeds by bringing them into the light.

John 17:20–23 – Jesus prays for unity among His followers.

Acts 17:26–30 – All nations made from one blood, called to repentance.

Romans 10:12–13 – "There is no difference between Jew and Gentile… the same Lord is Lord of all."

Romans 11:17–18 – Gentiles (Japheth) grafted into Israel's olive tree (Shem).

Ephesians 2:14–16 – Christ is our peace, destroying the dividing wall of hostility.

Ephesians 6:12 – Our struggle is against principalities and powers, not flesh and blood.

Galatians 3:28 – "There is neither Jew nor Gentile, slave nor free, male nor female, for you are all one in Christ Jesus."

Revelation 5:9–10 – Every tribe, tongue, people, and nation redeemed by the Lamb.

Revelation 7:9–10 – A great multitude of all nations standing before God in worship.

An Important Note on the Use of AI-Assisted Editing Tools

In the meticulous process of bringing this manuscript to life, I employed advanced AI-assisted editing tools. It is crucial to understand their role: they served as a modern-day editor, meticulously refining grammar, punctuation, and syntactical flow to ensure the manuscript's clarity, precision, and persuasive power. These tools did not—and could not—create the substance of this work.

The content, the theological insights, and the deeply personal reflections you find within these pages are the exclusive product of my own study, prayer, and a lifetime of lived experience. Every argument is born from my intellectual and spiritual journey. Every external source referenced has been properly and transparently cited, and no AI-generated content was ever used to replace original thought or research.

This statement is included to uphold the highest standard of integrity and transparency, affirming that while the medium may be modern, the message is authentic, original, and from the heart of a servant dedicated to the Kingdom of God.

Apostle K. M. Byam-Brown, Sr.

Apostle K.M. Byam-Brown, Sr. is a prophetic voice and seasoned Christian leader whose ministry is a testament to the relentless advance of the Kingdom of God. As a senior pastor, apostle, and scholar, his work transcends traditional boundaries, driven by a profound commitment to missiology—the strategic study of missionary work—and the development of innovative models that empower churches to thrive globally and locally.

Apostle Byam-Brown is a prolific author, having penned impactful works such as *Manifesting the Glory* and *The Rise of the Kingdom Runner*, which serve as essential guides for spiritual growth, Kingdom living, and a call to radical discipleship. His leadership is anchored in the founding and guidance of organizations like Kingdom Life International Assembly and the Global Alliance of Churches Networking to Advance the Kingdom of God (GACNAK). Through these alliances, he champions unity, fosters resource sharing, and cultivates a culture of Kingdom principles across diverse church communities worldwide.

In every facet of his multifaceted ministry—as a pastor, apostle, educator, and author—Apostle Byam-Brown is a catalyst for change, relentlessly equipping the Church to fulfill the Great Commission with a divine blend of innovation, spiritual authority, and cultural sensitivity.

www.ingramcontent.com/pod-product-compliance
Lightning Source LLC
Chambersburg PA
CBHW051214120626
46547CB00013B/1342